CAREER IDEAS
for kids who like
SCIENCE

THE CAREER IDEAS FOR KIDS SERIES

CAREER IDEAS
for kids who like
SCIENCE

Second Edition

DIANE LINDSEY REEVES
with
LINDSEY CLASEN

Illustrations by
NANCY BOND

Checkmark Books®
An imprint of Infobase Publishing

CAREER IDEAS FOR KIDS WHO LIKE SCIENCE, Second Edition

Checkmark Books
An imprint of Infobase Publishing, Inc.
132 West 31st Street
New York NY 10001

Library of Congress Cataloging-in-Publication Data

Reeves, Diane Lindsey, 1959–
  Career ideas for kids who like science. — 2nd ed. / Diane Lindsey Reeves with Lindsey Clasen; illustrations by Nancy Bond.
    p. cm — (The career ideas for kids series)
  Rev. ed. of: Science. 1998.
  Includes bibliographical references and index.
  ISBN-13: 978-0-8160-6549-3 (hc : alk. paper)
  ISBN-10: 0-8160-6549-7 (hc : alk. paper)
  ISBN-13: 978-0-8160-6550-9 (pbk : alk. paper)
  ISBN-10: 0-8160-6550-0 (pbk : alk. paper) 1. Science—Vocational guidance—Juvenile literature. I. Clasen, Lindsey. II. Reeves, Diane Lindsey, 1959– Science. III. Title. VI. Series.
  Q147.R38 2007
  502'.3—dc22   2007003593

Checkmark Books are available at special discounts when purchased in bulk quantities for businesses, associations, institutions, or sales promotions. Please call our Special Sales Department in New York at (212) 967-8800 or (800) 322-8755.

You can find Facts On File on the World Wide Web at http://www.factsonfile.com

Original text and cover design by Smart Graphics
Illustrations by Nancy Bond

Printed in the United States of America

MP Hermitage 10 9 8 7 6 5 4 3 2 1

This book is printed on acid-free paper.

CONTENTS

A million thanks to the people who took the time to share their career stories and provide photos for this book:

Gibor Basri
Michael Blackwell
Leslie Bonci
Anthony Conte
Carol Ellick
Ben Halpern
Henry C. Lee
Richard Lefebvre
Rose Lindsey
Ellen Molner
John Morales
Julius Nuccio
Ben Page
Roger Townley
Steve Spangler

Finally, much appreciation and admiration is due to all the behind-the-scenes people at Ferguson who have done so much to make this series all that it is. With extra thanks to James Chambers and Sarah Fogarty.

MAKE A CHOICE!

Choices.

You make them every day. What do I want for break-fast? Which shirt can I pull out of the dirty-clothes hamper to wear to school today? Should I finish my homework or play video games?

Some choices don't make much difference in the over-all scheme of things. Face it; who really cares whether you wear the blue shirt or the red one?

Other choices are a major big deal. Figuring out what you want to be when you grow up is one of those all-important choices.

But, you say, you're just a kid. How are you supposed to know what you want to do with your life?

You're right: 10, 11, 12, and even 13 are a bit young to know exactly what and where and how you're going to do whatever it is you're going to do as an adult. But it's the perfect time to start making some important discoveries about who you are, what you like to do, and what you do best. It's a great time to start exploring the options and experimenting with different ideas. In fact, there's never a better time to mess around with differ-ent career ideas without messing up your life.

When it comes to picking a career, you've basically got two choices.

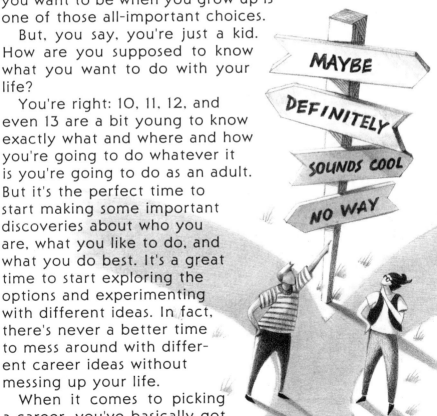

CHOICE A

You can be like lots of other people and just go with the flow. Float through school doing only what you absolutely have to in order to graduate, take any job you can find, collect a paycheck, and meander your way to retirement without making much of a splash in life.

Although many people take this route and do just fine, others end up settling for second best. They miss out on a meaningful education, satisfying work, and the rewards of a focused and well-planned career. That's why this path is not an especially good idea for someone who actually wants to have a life.

CHOICE B

Other people get a little more involved in choosing a career. They figure out what they want to accomplish in their lives—whether it's making a difference, making lots of money, or simply enjoying what they do. Then they find out what it takes to reach that goal, and set about doing it with gusto. It's kind of like these people do things on purpose instead of letting life happen by accident.

Choosing A is like going to an ice cream parlor where there are all kinds of awesome flavors and ordering a single scoop of plain vanilla. Going with Choice B is more like visiting that same ice cream parlor and ordering a super duper brownie sundae drizzled with hot fudge, smothered in whip cream, and topped with a big red cherry.

Do you see the difference?

Reading this book is a great idea for kids who want to go after life in a big way. It provides a first step toward learning about careers that match your skills, values, and dreams. It will help you make the most out of your time in school and maybe even inspire you to—as the U.S. Army so proudly says—"be all that you can be."

Ready for the challenge of Choice B? If so, read the next section for instructions on how to get started.

HOW TO USE THIS BOOK

This book isn't just about interesting careers that other people have. It's also a book about interesting careers that you can have.

Of course, it won't do you a bit of good to just read this book. To get the whole shebang, you're going to have to jump in with both feet, roll up your sleeves, put on your thinking cap—whatever it takes—to help you do these three things:

💡 Discover what you do best and enjoy the most. (This is the secret ingredient for finding work that's perfect for you.)

- Explore ways to match your interests and abilities with career ideas.
- Experiment with lots of different ideas until you find the ideal career. (It's like trying on all kinds of hats to see which ones fit!)

Use this book as a road map to some exciting career destinations. Here's what to expect in the chapters that follow.

GET IN GEAR!

First stop: discover. These activities will help you uncover important clues about the special traits and abilities that make you *you*. When you are finished you will have developed a personal Skill Set that will help guide you to career ideas in the next chapter.

TAKE A TRIP!

Next stop: explore. Cruise down the career idea highway and find out about a variety of career ideas that are especially appropriate for people who like science. Use the Skill Set chart at the beginning of each career profile to match your own interests with those required for success on the job.

Once you've identified a career that interests you, kick your exploration into high gear by checking out some of the Web sites, library resources, and professional organizations listed at the end of each career profile. For an extra challenge, follow the instructions for the Try It Out activities.

MAKE A SCIENTIFIC DETOUR!

Here's your chance to explore up-and-coming opportunities in environmental and technology sciences as well as the tried-and-true fields of research, medicine, and basic, hard-core sciences.

Just when you thought you'd seen it all, here come dozens of interesting science ideas to add to the career mix. Charge up your career search by learning all you can about some of these opportunities.

DON'T STOP NOW!

Third stop: experiment. The library, the telephone, a computer, and a mentor—four keys to a successful career planning adventure. Use them well, and before long you'll be on the trail of some hot career ideas of your own.

WHAT'S NEXT?

Make a plan! Chart your course (or at least the next stop) with these career planning road maps. Whether you're moving full steam ahead with a great idea or get slowed down at a yellow light of indecision, these road maps will keep you moving forward toward a great future.

Use a pencil—you're bound to make a detour or two along the way. But, hey, you've got to start somewhere.

HOORAY! YOU DID IT!

Some final rules of the road before sending you off to new adventures.

SOME FUTURE DESTINATIONS

This section lists a few career planning tools you'll want to know about.

You've got a lot of ground to cover in this phase of your career planning journey. Start your engines and get ready for an exciting adventure!

GET IN GEAR!

Career planning is a lifelong journey. There's usually more than one way to get where you're going, and there are often some interesting detours along the way. But you have to start somewhere. So rev up and find out all you can about one-of-a-kind, specially designed you. That's the first stop on what can be the most exciting trip of your life!

To get started, complete the five exercises described throughout the following pages.

DISCOVER #1: WATCH FOR SIGNS ALONG THE WAY

Road signs help drivers figure out how to get where they want to go. They provide clues about direction, road conditions, and safety. Your career road signs will provide clues about who you are, what you like, and what you do best. These clues can help you decide where to look for the career ideas that are best for you.

Complete the following statements to make them true for you. There are no right or wrong answers. Jot down the response that describes you best. Your answers will provide important clues about career paths you should explore.

Please Note: If this book does not belong to you, write your responses on a separate sheet of paper.

On my last report card, I got the best grade in _____ .

On my last report card, I got the worst grade in _____ .

I am happiest when _____ .

Something I can do for hours without getting bored is _____ .

Something that bores me out of my mind is _____ .

My favorite class is _____ .

My least favorite class is _____ .

The one thing I'd like to accomplish with my life is _____ .

My favorite thing to do after school is _____ .

My least favorite thing to do after school is _____ .

Something I'm really good at is _____ .

Something really tough for me to do is _____ .

My favorite adult person is _____ because _____ .

When I grow up _____ .

The kinds of books I like to read are about _____ .

The kinds of videos I like to watch are about _____ .

DISCOVER #2: RULES OF THE ROAD

Pretty much any job you can think of involves six common ingredients. Whether the work requires saving the world or selling bananas, all work revolves around a central **purpose** or reason for existing. All work is conducted somewhere, in some **place**, whether it's on the 28th floor of a city sky-scraper or on a cruise ship in the middle of an ocean. All work requires a certain **time** commitment and is performed using various types of **tools. People** also play an important part in most jobs—whether the job involves interacting with lots or very few of them. And, especially from where you are sitting as a kid still in school, all work involves some type of **preparation** to learn how to do the job.

Another word for these six common ingredients is *values*. Each one represents important aspects of work that people value in different ways. The following activity will give you a chance to think about what matters most to you in each of these areas. That way you'll get a better idea of things to look for as you explore different careers.

Here's how the process works:

First, read the statements listed for each value on the fol-lowing pages. Decide which, if any, represent your idea of an ideal job.

Next, take a look at the grid on page 16. For every value statement with which you agreed, draw its symbol in the appropriate space on your grid. (If this book doesn't belong to you, use a blank sheet of paper to draw your own grid with six big spaces.) Or, if you want to get really fancy, cut pic-tures out of magazines and glue them into the appropriate space. If you do not see a symbol that represents your best answer, make up a new one and sketch it in the appropriate box.

When you are finished, you'll have a very useful picture of the kinds of values that matter most to you in your future job.

PURPOSE Which of the following statements describes what you most hope to accomplish in your future work? Pick as many as are true for you and feel free to add others.		
♥	❏	I want to help other people.
💵	❏	I want to make lots of money.
★	❏	I want to do something I really believe in.
✋	❏	I want to make things.
🧠	❏	I want to use my brain power in challenging ways.
💡	❏	I want to work with my own creative ideas.
🏆	❏	I want to be very successful.
	❏	I want to find a good company and stick with it for the rest of my life.
	❏	I want to be famous.
Other purpose-related things that are especially important to me are		

PLACE

When you think about your future work, what kind of place would you most like to do it in? Pick as many as are true for you and feel free to add others.

	❏	I want to work in a big city skyscraper.
	❏	I want to work in a shopping mall or retail store.
	❏	I want to work in the great outdoors.
	❏	I want to travel a lot for my work.
	❏	I want to work out of my own home.
	❏	I want to work for a government agency.
	❏	I want to work in a school or university.
	❏	I want to work in a factory or laboratory.

Other place-related things that are especially important to me are

TIME

When you think about your future work, what kind of schedule sounds most appealing to you? Pick as many as are true for you and feel free to add others.

	❑	I'd rather work regular business hours—nine to five, Monday through Friday.
	❑	I'd like to have lots of vacation time.
	❑	I'd prefer a flexible schedule so I can balance my work, family, and personal needs.
	❑	I'd like to work nights only so my days are free.
	❑	I'd like to work where the pace is fast and I stay busy all day.
	❑	I'd like to work where I would always know exactly what I'm supposed to do.
	❑	I'd like to work where I could plan my own day.
	❑	I'd like to work where there's lots of variety and no two days are alike.

Other time-related things that are especially important to me are

TOOLS

What kinds of things would you most like to work with? Pick as many as are true for you and feel free to add others.

	❏	I'd prefer to work mostly with people.
	❏	I'd prefer to work mostly with technology.
	❏	I'd prefer to work mostly with machines.
	❏	I'd prefer to work mostly with products people buy.
	❏	I'd prefer to work mostly with planes, trains, automobiles, or other things that go.
	❏	I'd prefer to work mostly with ideas.
	❏	I'd prefer to work mostly with information.
	❏	I'd prefer to work mostly with nature.

Other tool-related things that are especially important to me are

PEOPLE

What role do other people play in your future work? How many do you want to interact with on a daily basis? What age group would you most enjoy working with? Pick as many as are true for you and feel free to add others.

	❏	I'd like to work with lots of people all day long.
	❏	I'd prefer to work alone most of the time.
	❏	I'd like to work as part of a team.
	❏	I'd like to work with people I might choose as friends.
	❏	I'd like to work with babies, children, or teenagers,
	❏	I'd like to work mostly with elderly people.
	❏	I'd like to work mostly with people who are in trouble.
	❏	I'd like to work mostly with people who are ill.

Other people-related things that are especially important to me are

PREPARATION

When you think about your future work, how much time and energy do you want to devote to preparing for it? Pick as many as are true for you and feel free to add others.

	❑	I want to find a job that requires a college degree.
	❑	I want to find a job where I could learn what I need to know on the job.
	❑	I want to find a job that requires no additional train-ing after I graduate from high school.
	❑	I want to find a job where the more education I get, the bet-ter my chances for a better job.
BOSS	❑	I want to run my own business and be my own boss.
Other preparation-related things that are especially impor-tant to me are		

Now that you've uncovered some word clues about the types of values that are most important to you, use the grid on the following page (or use a separate sheet of paper if this book does not belong to you) to "paint a picture" of your ideal future career. Use the icons as ideas for how to visualize each statement. Or, if you'd like to get really creative, get a large sheet of paper, some markers, magazines, and glue or tape and create a collage.

PURPOSE	PLACE	TIME
TOOLS	**PEOPLE**	**PREPARATION**

DISCOVER #3: DANGEROUS DETOURS

Half of figuring out what you do want to do is figuring out what you don't want to do. Get a jump start on this process by making a list of 10 careers you already know you absolutely don't want to do.

Warning: Failure to heed early warning signs to avoid careers like this can result in long hours of boredom and frustration spent doing a job you just weren't meant to do.

(If this book does not belong to you, make your list on a separate sheet of paper.)

1. _____   _____

2. _____   _____

3. _____   _____

4. _____   _____

5. _____   _____

6. _____   _____

7. _____   _____

8. _____   _____

9. _____   _____

10. _____

Red Flag Summary:
Look over your list, and in the second column above (or on a separate sheet of paper) see if you can summarize what it is about these jobs that makes you want to avoid them like a bad case of cooties.

DISCOVER #4: ULTIMATE CAREER DESTINATION

Imagine that your dream job is like a favorite tourist destination, and you have to convince other people to pick it over every other career in the world. How would you describe it? What features make it especially appealing to you? What does a person have to do to have a career like it?

Take a blank sheet of paper and fold it into thirds. Fill each column on both sides with words and pictures that create a vivid image of what you'd most like your future career to be.

Special note: Just for now, instead of actually naming a specific career, describe what your ideal career would be like. In places where the name of the career would be used, leave a blank space like this _____. For instance: For people who want to become rich and famous, being a _____ is the way to go.

DISCOVER #5: GET SOME DIRECTION

It's easy to get lost when you don't have a good idea of where you want to go. This is especially true when you start thinking about what to do with the rest of your life. Unless you focus on where you want to go, you might get lost or even miss the exit. This discover exercise will help you connect your own interests and abilities with a whole world of career opportunities.

Mark the activities that you enjoy doing or would enjoy doing if you had the chance. Be picky. Don't mark ideas that you wish you would do. Mark only those that you would really do. For instance, if skydiving sounds appealing but you'd never do it because you are terrified of heights, don't mark it.

Please Note: If this book does not belong to you, write your responses on a separate sheet of paper.

- ❏ 1. Rescue a cat stuck in a tree
- ❏ 2. Visit the pet store every time you go to the mall
- ❏ 3. Paint a mural on the cafeteria wall
- ❏ 4. Run for student council
- ❏ 5. Send e-mail to a "pen pal" in another state
- ❏ 6. Survey your classmates to find out what they do after school
- ❏ 7. Try out for the school play
- ❏ 8. Dissect a frog and identify the different organs
- ❏ 9. Play baseball, soccer, football, or _____ (fill in your favorite sport)

❏ 10. Talk on the phone to just about anyone who will talk back

❏ 11. Try foods from all over the world—Thailand, Poland, Japan, etc.

❏ 12. Write poems about things that are happening in your life

❏ 13. Create a really scary haunted house to take your friends through on Halloween

❏ 14. Recycle all your family's trash

❏ 15. Bake a cake and decorate it for your best friend's birthday

❏ 16. Sell enough advertisements for the school yearbook to win a trip to Walt Disney World

❏ 17. Simulate an imaginary flight through space on your computer screen

❏ 18. Build model airplanes, boats, doll houses, or anything from kits

❏ 19. Teach your friends a new dance routine

❏ 20. Watch the stars come out at night and see how many constellations you can find

❏ 21. Watch baseball, soccer, football, or _____ (fill in your favorite sport) on TV

❏ 22. Give a speech in front of the entire school

❏ 23. Plan the class field trip to Washington, D.C.

❏ 24. Read everything in sight, including the back of the cereal box

❏ 25. Figure out "who dunnit" in a mystery story

❏ 26. Take in stray or hurt animals

❏ 27. Make a poster announcing the school football game

❏ 28. Think up a new way to make the lunch line move faster and explain it to the cafeteria staff

❏ 29. Put together a multimedia show for a school assembly using music and lots of pictures and graphics

❏ 30. Invest your allowance in the stock market and keep track of how it does

❏ 31. Go to the ballet or opera every time you get the chance

❏ 32. Do experiments with a chemistry set

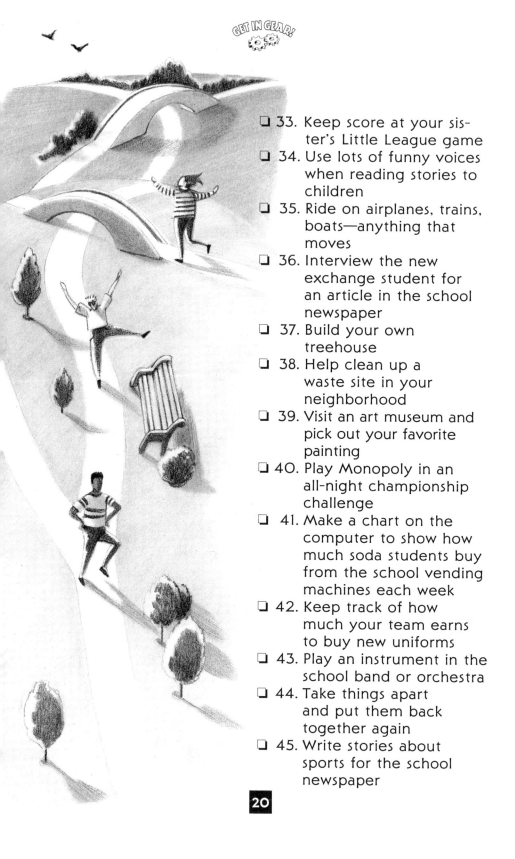

❑ 33. Keep score at your sister's Little League game

❑ 34. Use lots of funny voices
when reading stories to
children

❑ 35. Ride on airplanes, trains,
boats—anything that
moves

❑ 36. Interview the new
exchange student for
an article in the school
newspaper

❑ 37. Build your own
treehouse

❑ 38. Help clean up a
waste site in your
neighborhood

❑ 39. Visit an art museum and
pick out your favorite
painting

❑ 40. Play Monopoly in an
all-night championship
challenge

❑ 41. Make a chart on the
computer to show how
much soda students buy
from the school vending
machines each week

❑ 42. Keep track of how
much your team earns
to buy new uniforms

❑ 43. Play an instrument in the
school band or orchestra

❑ 44. Take things apart
and put them back
together again

❑ 45. Write stories about
sports for the school
newspaper

❏ 46. Listen to other people talk about their problems
❏ 47. Imagine yourself in exotic places
❏ 48. Hang around bookstores and libraries
❏ 49. Play harmless practical jokes on April Fools' Day
❏ 50. Join the 4-H club at your school
❏ 51. Take photographs at the school talent show
❏ 52. Make money by setting up your own business—
paper route, lemonade stand, etc.
❏ 53. Create an imaginary city using a computer
❏ 54. Do 3-D puzzles
❏ 55. Keep track of the top 10 songs of the week
❏ 56. Read about famous inventors and their inventions
❏ 57. Make play-by-play announcements at the school
football game
❏ 58. Answer the phones during a telethon to raise
money for orphans
❏ 59. Be an exchange student in another country
❏ 60. Write down all your secret thoughts and favorite
sayings in a journal
❏ 61. Jump out of an airplane (with a parachute, of course)

❑ 62. Plant and grow a garden in your backyard (or windowsill)

❑ 63. Use a video camera to make your own movies

❑ 64. Get your friends together to help clean up your town after a hurricane

❑ 65. Spend your summer at a computer camp learning lots of new computer programs

❑ 66. Build bridges, skyscrapers, and other structures out of LEGOs

❑ 67. Plan a concert in the park for little kids

❑ 68. Collect different kinds of rocks

❑ 69. Help plan a sports tournament

❑ 70. Be DJ for the school dance

❑ 71. Learn how to fly a plane or sail a boat

❑ 72. Write funny captions for pictures in the school yearbook

❑ 73. Scuba dive to search for buried treasure

❑ 74. Recognize and name several different breeds of cats, dogs, and other animals

❑ 75. Sketch pictures of your friends

❏ 76. Pick out neat stuff to sell at the school store
❏ 77. Answer your classmates' questions about how to use the computer
❏ 78. Draw a map showing how to get to your house from school
❏ 79. Make up new words to your favorite songs
❏ 80. Take a hike and name the different kinds of trees, birds, or flowers
❏ 81. Referee intramural basketball games
❏ 82. Join the school debate team
❏ 83. Make a poster with postcards from all the places you went on your summer vacation
❏ 84. Write down stories that your grandparents tell you about when they were young

CALCULATE THE CLUES

Now is your chance to add it all up. Each of the 12 boxes on the following pages contains an interest area that is common to both your world and the world of work. Follow these directions to discover your personal Skill Set:

1. Find all of the numbers that you checked on pages 18–23 in the following boxes and mark

them with an X. Work your way all the way through number 84.

2. Go back and count the Xs marked for each interest area. Write that number in the space that says "Total."

3. Find the interest area with the highest total and put a number one in the "Rank" blank of that box. Repeat this process for the next two highest scoring areas. Rank the second highest as number two and the third highest as number three.

4. If you have more than three strong areas, choose the three that are most important and interesting to you.

Remember: If this book does not belong to you, write your responses on a separate sheet of paper.

ADVENTURE
- ❏ 1
- ❏ 13
- ❏ 25
- ❏ 37
- ❏ 49
- ❏ 61
- ❏ 73

Total: _____
Rank: _____

ANIMALS & NATURE
- ❏ 2
- ❏ 14
- ❏ 26
- ❏ 38
- ❏ 50
- ❏ 62
- ❏ 74

Total: _____
Rank: _____

ART
- ❏ 3
- ❏ 15
- ❏ 27
- ❏ 39
- ❏ 51
- ❏ 63
- ❏ 75

Total: _____
Rank: _____

BUSINESS

- ❏ 4
- ❏ 16
- ❏ 28
- ❏ 40
- ❏ 52
- ❏ 64
- ❏ 76

Total: _____

Rank: _____

COMPUTERS

- ❏ 5
- ❏ 17
- ❏ 29
- ❏ 41
- ❏ 53
- ❏ 65
- ❏ 77

Total: _____

Rank: _____

MATH

- ❏ 6
- ❏ 18
- ❏ 30
- ❏ 42
- ❏ 54
- ❏ 66
- ❏ 78

Total: _____

Rank: _____

MUSIC/DANCE

- ❏ 7
- ❏ 19
- ❏ 31
- ❏ 43
- ❏ 55
- ❏ 67
- ❏ 79

Total: _____

Rank: _____

SCIENCE

- ❏ 8
- ❏ 20
- ❏ 32
- ❏ 44
- ❏ 56
- ❏ 68
- ❏ 80

Total: _____

Rank: _____

SPORTS

- ❏ 9
- ❏ 21
- ❏ 33
- ❏ 45
- ❏ 57
- ❏ 69
- ❏ 81

Total: _____

Rank: _____

TALKING

- ❏ 10
- ❏ 22
- ❏ 34
- ❏ 46
- ❏ 58
- ❏ 70
- ❏ 82

Total: _____

Rank: _____

TRAVEL

- ❏ 11
- ❏ 23
- ❏ 35
- ❏ 47
- ❏ 59
- ❏ 71
- ❏ 83

Total: _____

Rank: _____

WRITING

- ❏ 12
- ❏ 24
- ❏ 36
- ❏ 48
- ❏ 60
- ❏ 72
- ❏ 84

Total: _____

Rank: _____

What are your top three interest areas? List them here (or on a separate piece of paper).

1. _____

2. _____

3. _____

This is your personal Skill Set and provides important clues about the kinds of work you're most likely to enjoy. Remember it and look for career ideas with a Skill Set that matches yours most closely. You'll find a Skill Set box at the beginning of each career profile in the following section.

TAKE A TRIP!

Cruise down the career idea highway and enjoy in-depth profiles of some of the interesting options in this field. Keep in mind all that you've discovered about yourself so far. Find the careers that match your own Skill Set first. After that, keep on trucking through the other ideas—exploration is the name of this game.

You'll probably notice that many of the careers in this book require a combined knowledge of science and math. That's because math is the language of science. If you don't know math, you can't "speak" science. If a scientific field is in your future, count on taking some fairly heavy-duty math courses, too. Add this element to the equation as you start your trip down Scientific Opportunity Avenue.

You may also notice that many of these professions require college degrees, master's degrees, or higher. Education, and plenty of it, is one of the main routes to many traditional scientific careers. It makes sense that in a field based on many complex, unchangeable laws, the more you know about the laws, the more you can do in the field.

However, if you love science but don't love the idea of spending years in school, don't despair! There's usually more than one way to get just about anywhere. Sometimes you just have to be a little more creative.

One path to a scientific career without a college degree leads to a single word: technician. Behind every full-fledged scientist is a good technician assisting in a variety of interesting and invaluable ways. Make technician your final destination or a pitstop on the way to other things.

Meanwhile, as you read about the following careers, imagine yourself doing each job and ask yourself the following questions:

- ☼ Would I like it?
- ☼ Would I be good at it?
- ☼ Is it the stuff my career dreams are made of?

If so, make a quick exit to explore what it involves, try it out, check it out, and get acquainted. Look out for the symbols below.

Buckle up and enjoy the trip!

 **TRY IT OUT**

 **CHECK IT OUT**

 **ON THE WEB**

 AT THE LIBRARY

 WITH THE EXPERTS

A NOTE ON WEB SITES

Internet sites tend to move around the Web a bit. If you have trouble finding a particular site, use an Internet browser to find a specific Web site or type of information.

Archaeologist

SHORTCUTS

GO visit natural history museums.

READ *National Geographic Kids* magazine online at http://www.nationalgeographic.com/kids.

TRY investigating the past—dig up all the information you can about Native Americans, the Aztecs, early American settlers, or another group of interest.

SKILL SET

✔ SCIENCE

✔ ANIMALS & NATURE

✔ TRAVEL

WHAT IS AN ARCHAEOLOGIST?

An archaeologist is part researcher, part historian, part investigator. He or she must be handy with a shovel and pick. These are the bare bones basics of an archaeologist's work. Archaeologists gather information and recover data that link the past with the present. Everything they do centers around answering three questions about the people who once inhabited each excavation site: Who lived here? How did they live? What was life like?

Archaeology is actually a subfield of anthropology. While archaeology is the study of what people leave behind, anthropology is

the study of people and their behavior. Three other subfields combine to create a full picture of life in the past. One of these is linguistics—the study of language; another is physical anthropology—the study of human remains; and the third one is cultural anthropology—the study of modern-day cultures and peoples.

All four disciplines fit together like pieces of a puzzle. Scientists generally specialize in one area and work with collegues from the other areas to make well-rounded conclusions about their findings. Count on all four areas being part of your course of study if you pursue either the field of archaeology or the field of anthropology.

Archaeology is the systematic recovery of evidence of human life in the past. Physical objects or artifacts such as art and tools provide clues about life as it used to be. An archaeologist researches, excavates, preserves, studies, and classifies artifacts to develop a picture of how people lived in earlier cultures and societies.

Archaeological fieldwork is conducted all over the world, often in remote areas, and can be as diverse in nature as tracing the paths of ancient hunter-gatherers or reconstructing the lives and times of early American settlers. Recovering this data can be a painstaking process as these historic finds are often deeply buried in the ground, covered by later civilizations. Archaeologists work carefully and skillfully to remove objects and record their relationship to each other. A thorough cleaning, cataloging, and analysis is systematically conducted on each object as archaeologists figure out how to fit their findings into the broad scheme of human history.

Many archaeologists are employed at colleges and universities and teach at least part time between projects. Others work for government agencies such as the U.S. Forest Service or for private industry. Archaeology is a relatively small field with professionals marked by a common passion for making new discoveries. Those who continue to thrive (that is, "make a good living") in this field are the ones who find creative ways to combine their interest in archaeology with other skills in greater demand (see the Get Acquainted profile for a great example of this).

☞ TRY IT OUT

TIME CAPSULE

Do your part for the archaeologists of the future. Prepare a time capsule and bury it in your backyard for archaeologists to find in some distant century. Think about the kinds of objects that would provide the most telling evidence about our society, wrap each item in current newspapers, and place them in an airtight container (beg one of those plastic containers from the kitchen) and dig away. Make sure you get permission before you dig!

If a century or two seems too long to wait, make a date to dig it up yourself after some momentous occasion—graduation from college, the birth of your first child (yikes!), or whatever.

HAVE SHOVEL, WILL TRAVEL

If you've really caught the archaeology bug, you won't be content to just read about all these discoveries for long. Eventually, you'll want to see things for yourself. Opportunities abound for forays into the past.

First, find out what's happening in your own backyard (or at least nearby). Three sources of local information include the following:

- Your local chapter of the Archaeological Institute of America (http://www.archaeological.org).
- Your state's historic preservation office. Every state has one. Check the phone book for the office in your state.
- Natural history or living history museums in your area. Be sure to ask the curator or tour guide for tips on other exhibits or projects in the area. You never know until you ask!
- Call the Passport in Time Clearinghouse at 800-281-9176 to get information about archaeological and historic preservation projects sponsored by the U.S. Forest

Service. These projects are supervised by professional archaeologists but open for public participation. Make sure to ask them to add your name to their mailing list—they send out a newsletter twice a year that is full of information about interesting projects.

Keep digging—there is lots of exciting work being done in this field.

 CHECK IT OUT

ON THE WEB

Here are some addresses for fascinating online archaeology sites on the World Wide Web.

HIGH-TECH DIGS

- Get your hands dirty online at the Archaeology Interactive Dig Web site at http://www.archaeology.org/interactive.
- Explore *Dig*, the archaeology magazine for kids at http://www.digonsite.com.
- See what you can find at the National Park Service Archaeology for Kids Web site at http://www.cr.nps.gov/archeology/public/kids/index.htm.
- Visit the Crow Canyon Archaeology Center at http://www.crowcanyon.org/kids.html.
- Take a virtual tour of the Smithsonian museums at http://www.smithsonianeducation.org/students.
- Find links to all kinds of cool archaeology Web sites for kids at http://www.digonsite.com.

To find out how you can get involved in real archaeological digs, visit these Web sites:

- Passport in Time at http://www.passportintime.com
- Society for American Archaeology at http://www.saa.org

📚 AT THE LIBRARY

DIG UP SOME GOOD BOOKS

Dig into some of these books about archaeology:

Fagan, Brian. *Archaeologists: Explorers of the Human Past.* New York: Oxford University Press, 2003.

McIntosh, Jane. *Eyewitness: Archeology.* New York: DK Publishing, 2000.

Orna-Ornstein, John. *Archaeology: Discovering the Past.* New York: Oxford University Press, 2002.

Panchyk, Richard. *Archaeology for Kids: Uncovering the Mysteries of Our Past.* Chicago: Chicago Review Press, 2001.

Robinson, Tony. *Archaeology.* Boston: Kingfisher Publications, 2004.

For a whirlwind tour of the ancient world, try some of these titles in the *National Geographic Investigates* series:

Ball, Jacqueline. *National Geographic Investigates: Ancient China.* Washington, D.C.: National Geographic, 2006.

Gruber, Beth. *National Geographic Investigates: Ancient Iraq.* Washington, D.C.: National Geographic, 2007.

Rubalcaba, Jill. *National Geographic Investigates: Ancient Egypt.* Washington, D.C.: National Geographic, 2006.

Just for fun, book a virtual trip with the Good Times Travel Agency and enjoy some fictional adventures in titles such as:

Bailey, Linda. *Adventures in the Ice Age.* Tonawanda, New York: Kids Can Press, 2004.

———. *Adventures in the Middle Ages.* Tonawanda, New York: Kids Can Press, 2000.

———. *Adventures with the Vikings.* Tonawanda, New York: Kids Can Press, 2001.

☙ WITH THE EXPERTS

Archaeological Institute of
America
656 Beacon Street, 6th Floor
Boston, MA 02215-2006
http://www.archaeological.org

EARTHWATCH Institute
Three Clock Tower Place,
Suite 100
Maynard, MA 01754-2574
http://www.earthwatch.org

Smithsonian Center for Education
and Museum Studies
PO Box 37012
SI Building, Room 153, MRC 010
Washington DC 20013-7102
http://museumstudies.si.edu

Society for American Archaeology
900 Second Street NE, Suite 12
Washington, DC 20002-3560
http://www.saa.org

GET ACQUAINTED

Carol J. Ellick, Archaeologist

CAREER PATH

CHILDHOOD ASPIRATION:
To be an artist, because everyone
told her she was good at drawing.

FIRST JOB: Picking through
people's garbage (really!) as
part of The Garbage Project
at University of Arizona. Gross
as it sounds, it was part of an
anthropological study about
modern day life.

CURRENT JOB: Director of outreach and education at the SRI Foundation, a nonprofit organization dedicated to advancing historic preservation
through education, training, and research.

THE DEFINING MOMENT

Carol Ellick was lucky. She knew what she wanted and she
knew how to get it. Well, sort of. Actually, she's had the pluck

and imagination to link a string of seemingly unrelated interests and occurrences into a fascinating archaeological career
spanning over 25 years.

When she was 14 years old, her family took a cross-country
trip to Mesa Verde in Colorado to see the cliff dwellings.
While there, they visited a little museum. Things clicked for
her when she saw a big pot lying on its side with kernels
of corn falling out of it. The realization that this scene was
reconstructed from the home of a person who lived over
800 years ago was mind-boggling. It added the human factor
to the archaeological process and, although she didn't realize
it at the time, this was a turning point in her life.

ONE THING LEADS TO ANOTHER

She studied and dug and studied some more until she
received a degree in anthropology with an emphasis in
archaeology. After graduating, she spent the summer fighting fires with the Forest Service in Oregon—the hardest work
she's ever done in her life, she says. Although this particular
job had nothing to do with her chosen vocation, it led to a big
break in archaeology. While she was working there she met
the Forest Service's district archaeologist and talked to him
about the field. One thing lead to another. . . .

WHAT GOES AROUND, COMES AROUND

The Forest Service archaeologist asked her if she could draw
some pictures of artifacts that they had found. Could she
draw? Of course she could draw. She had been drawing great
sketches of people and objects since she was a child. She had
always wanted to be an artist. Ellick drew the sketches, was
offered a job as a scientific illustrator, and a career was born.
Almost as a fluke, Ellick was able to combine her two great talents and interests in life—art and archaeology—as a career.

AND THAT'S NOT ALL

While working as an archaeologist and illustrator, she also had
the chance to work with kids and teachers. One thing led to

another. She went back to school and obtained a master's degree in education. Now she actually has two jobs in one, since her work combines her skills as an archaeologist and an educator. Whether it's designing a brochure about an excavation site, creating a display for schools or museums, conducting site tours, or training teachers how to make archaeology come alive to their students, Ellick continues to perfect her niche as an archaeological artist.

ADVICE TO YOUNG ARCHAEOLOGISTS

Ellick has a daughter who is now in college. She encourages her daughter to explore what she wants and to make her own path. Good advice for you, too!

Astronomer

SKILL SET

✔ COMPUTERS

✔ MATH

✔ SCIENCE

WHAT IS AN ASTRONOMER?

Here's a riddle for you. Why is the oldest science also the youngest science? Astronomy is often considered the oldest science because it represents one of the earliest scientific activities of humankind. Since the beginning of recorded history, people have been looking to the stars for answers about the universe. Yet, it's also the youngest because year after year new discoveries are made that change ideas about the nature of the universe.

Astronomers use the principles of physics and mathematics to study the universe—the sun, moon, planets, stars, and galaxies. They study

objects millions and even billions of light-years away. Since you can't put a star in a test tube, they use complex computers and telescopes to do their work. Contrary to what you might expect, few astronomers spend more than a few days or nights per year working at a telescope. More time is spent at the computer—analyzing and interpreting data and writing research reports.

Astronomy is one profession you can't fake your way through. Either you love it with an all-consuming passion or you shouldn't be in the field. The combination of a quality education, ability, and genuine interest in the subject make it easier to find a job in a profession where there are often more job-seekers than jobs. Fortunately, the strenuous training involved in preparing for a career in astronomy also provides an excellent background for other fields such as optics, computer science, physics, and engineering.

The American Astronomical Society advises that "decisions made in high school can have a big effect on a science career. Students who take science and math courses after the tenth grade have the best chance of successfully pursuing a science or engineering career." Make sure precalculus, chemistry, and physics appear on your class schedule before you graduate.

Most astronomers work at universities or colleges where they often combine teaching and research responsibilities. About a third of astronomers work at national observatories or government laboratories such as NASA, the Naval Research Laboratory, the U.S. Naval Observatory, the National Radio Astronomy Observatory, the National Optical Astronomy Observatories, and the Space Telescope Science Institute. A smaller percentage work in business or the aerospace industry. Astronomers can also be found working in planetariums, science museums, secondary schools, or in the science journalism field.

Astronomers see the universe as a gigantic puzzle and try to put each piece together. How are your puzzle-working skills? Ready for the ultimate challenge?

👉 TRY IT OUT

SCIENCE FACT OR FICTION?

Following are astronomical discoveries made in the past two decades. Find out all you can about them at the library and on the Internet. Record your discoveries in a notebook designated just for science observation projects.

black holes	"great walls" of galaxies
brown dwarfs	light echoes around exploding stars
cosmic jets	pulsars
Einstein rings	quasars
gamma ray bursters	voids in space
gravitational lenses	

THE SKY IS THE LIMIT

Get better acquainted with the world outside your bedroom window with these two activities:

First, go online to http://www.fourmilab.ch/yoursky to create a map of the sky from wherever it is that you live. Once there, you'll find that you have two choices. Either you can enter the exact latitude and longitude of your hometown or you can select a nearby city from a list provided at the Web site. Once you have created the map, find the name of the nearest constellation. Use an Internet search engine such as Google or Yahoo to find information about the constellation. Use the sky map and any information you find to create a collage.

Second, make a model of the solar system using whatever materials you have on hand—colored markers and paper, papier mâché, or whatever. You'll find helpful information about which planets go where at Web sites such as:

- ☼ http://www.exploratorium.edu/ronh/solar_system
- ☼ http://www.nationalgeographic.com/solarsystem
- ☼ http://www.solarviews.com/eng/homepage.htm

 CHECK IT OUT

ON THE WEB

REV UP THE SEARCH ENGINE

You'll find a star-studded array of information about astronomy online at these Web sites:

- ☿ Find a beginner's guide to astronomy at http://www. dustbunny.com/afk.
- ☿ See some videos of space at http://www.space. com/spacewatch.
- ☿ Explore the Kid's Astronomy Web site at http://www. kidsastronomy.com.
- ☿ Observe more basic astronomy stuff at http://www. frontiernet.net/~kidpower/astronomy.html.
- ☿ Blast off to this interactive astronomy Web site: http://starchild.gsfc.nasa.gov/docs/StarChild.
- ☿ Ask the Space Scientist at http://image.gsfc.nasa. gov/poetry/ask/askmag.html.
- ☿ Take a virtual tour of the eight planets (and dwarf planet Pluto) at http://seds.lpl.arizona.edu/ nineplanets/nineplanets.
- ☿ Have some fun learning about space at the Space Place at http://spaceplace.nasa.gov/en/kids.

AT THE LIBRARY

OUT OF THIS WORLD READING

Do some space travel and star-gazing in books such as:

Bond, Peter. *DK Guide: Space.* New York: DK Publishing, 2006.

De Goursac, Olivier. *Space: Exploring the Moon, the Planets, and Beyond.* New York: Harry Abrams, 2006.

Doak, Robin S. *Galileo: Astronomer and Physicist.* Minneapolis, Minn.: Compass Point Books, 2005.

Gormley, Beatrice. *Maria Mitchell: The Soul of an Astronomer.* Grand Rapids, Mich.: Eerdmans Books for Young Readers, 2003.

Haydon, Julie. *Astronomers.* New York: Macmillan, 2004.

McCutcheon, Scott, and Bobbi McCutcheon. *Space and Astronomy: The People Behind the Science.* New York: Facts on File, 2006.

Solway, Andrew. *Quantum Leaps and Big Bangs: A History of Astronomy.* Chicago: Heinemann, 2005.

Stott, Carole. *The World of Astronomy.* Boston: Kingfisher, 2006.

Thomson, Sarah. *Extreme Stars.* New York: Harper Collins, 2006.

WITH THE EXPERTS

American Association of Variable Star Observers
49 Bay State Road
Cambridge, MA 02138-1203
http://www.aavso.org

American Astronomical Society
2000 Florida Avenue NW, Suite 400
Washington, DC 20009-1231
http://www.aas.org

Astronomical League
9201 Ward Parkway, Suite 100
Kansas City, MO 64114-3339
http://www.astroleague.org
(Ask about local amateur astronomy clubs! There are thousands of them around the country!)

NASA Goddard Space Flight Center
Public Inquiries
Mail Code 130
Greenbelt, MD 20771-0001
http://www.nasa.gov/centers/goddard/home

GET ACQUAINTED

Professor Gibor Basri,
Astronomer

CAREER PATH

CHILDHOOD ASPIRATION:
Ever since he was six years old working in astronomy was his goal. In eighth grade he did a career report and found out that astronomy wasn't a great choice because it's a small field. He started out studying physics in college but decided to "go for it" in graduate school.

FIRST JOB: Washing dishes in his college dormitory. He only lasted two weeks because he discovered too many inefficiencies, corrected them, and worked himself out of a pay-by-the-hour job.

CURRENT JOB: Professor of astronomy at the University of California teaching everything from introductory freshmen courses to very technical graduate seminars.

MOST EXCITING DISCOVERY (SO FAR)

Brown dwarfs are a celestial object somewhere between a planet and a star in size and brightness, and Basri announced the first brown dwarf ever to be authenticated in June 1995. Others have been discovered since then. Basri's discovery was made possible because of access to the University of California's Keck telescope—the world's largest telescope.

It took a while to get it right. The first test failed, and he had to backtrack to figure out why. It eventually became apparent that the star cluster containing the brown dwarf was older—and therefore fainter—than he had originally thought. His hard work and perseverance paid off in the end.

PUBLISH OR PERISH

With over 100 major research papers to his credit, Basri is in no danger of "perishing" in the academic world. Among his titles are "The Discovery of Brown Dwarfs" (*Scientific American*, April 2000), "What is a Planet?" (*Mercury*, December 2003), and "Brown Dwarfs: Cooler Than Cool" (*Sky & Telescope*, April 2005). You won't find these works at your local bookstore, but they represent important contributions to the study of the universe.

IS THERE LIFE ON OTHER PLANETS?

Basri says yes, bacterial life at the very least. And, with so many planets and galaxies left unexplored, who knows? maybe there really is such a thing as ETs. Expect someone (maybe you'll be the one) to discover life on another planet (possibly even life similar to what we know on Earth) in your lifetime.

BEST ADVICE FOR POTENTIAL ASTRONOMERS

Get on it early! Start taking as many science and math courses as you can beginning in junior high. It's easier to move out of science into other fields than it is to move into science from other fields. If you haven't established a good background in math and science by the end of high school, you're in trouble.

Chemist

SKILL SET

✔ COMPUTERS

✔ SCIENCE

✔ MATH

GO bake a cake and see for yourself what happens when you mix certain ingredients together.

READ *Dr. Jekyll and Mr. Hyde.* Written more than 100 years ago, it is a classic tale of chemistry run amok.

TRY making a list of all the chemicals you find in items around the house. Be sure to check the kitchen, the bathroom, and the garage.

WHAT IS A CHEMIST?

What does your body have in common with a compact disc, a book, a hockey puck, and a can of paint? They're all made out of chemicals. Chemists are the people who put chemicals together in various ways to create new products or solve specific problems.

Many chemists work in laboratories equipped with state-of-the-art (awesome) equipment. Their work can involve everything from developing everyday products like deodorant and makeup to looking for cures to diseases like AIDS. They also work to preserve and improve our food, air, and water.

Almost half of chemists work as researchers exploring new processes and developing or improving products. Following are descriptions of some chemistry specialties:

Agricultural chemists develop and test the chemicals used to aid crop production—herbicides, fungicides, and insecticides.

Environmental chemists look at how to protect our world from contaminants and pollution problems.

Materials scientists integrate applications from many scientific disciplines to develop products such as metals, ceramics, rubber, and paint.

Pharmaceutical chemists develop medicines using natural ingredients from plants and synthetic drug compounds.

Polymer chemists apply specialized technology to a variety of applications including plastics, adhesives, and biomedical products such as artificial skin and nicotine patches.

College is a must for anyone pursuing a career in this field. A two-year associate of arts degree prepares you for work as a chemical technician. Further education provides more advanced opportunities. The most successful chemists carefully blend a broad knowledge of the sciences with a highly focused specialty. As with any scientific endeavor, chemists must learn how to learn and to be adaptable to new technology and frequent advances in the field.

 TRY IT OUT

CHEMICAL DETECTIVE

Congratulations! You, the world's youngest chemist, have been hired to help your school get smart about chemicals and other environmental hazards. Go online to the Green Squad Web site at http://www.nrdc.org/greensquad/intro/intro_1.asp. Be sure to print out the checklist found at http://www.nrdc.org/greensquad/intro/progress.htm to include with your suggestions for ways to make your school "greener."

 CHECK IT OUT

ON THE WEB
MIX IT UP

Become a kitchen chemist! There are lots of online "recipes" you can try. Here are some Web sites to try.

- Accidental Scientist at http://www.exploratorium.com/cooking
- Countertop Chemistry at http://www.science_house.org/learn/CountertopChem/index.html
- Discovery Kitchen Chemistry at http://www.discoverychannel.co.uk/science/kitchen_chemistry
- Kitchen Chemistry at http://pbskids.org/zoom/games/kitchenchemistry
- Fun Food Stuff http://www.biotech.wisc.edu/Education/FunFoodStuff/default.htm

Remember to follow all instructions and be extremely careful. Some chemicals simply don't mix well with others. Be sure you know which ones are which BEFORE you mix them.

COMPUTER CHEMISTRY

The Internet comes through as an outstanding source of information for aspiring chemists. The following sites are full of resources and links to an incredible array of chemistry resources.

- Stop by the American Chemical Society's Web site for kids at http://www.chemistry.org/kids.
- Visit the National Atomic Museum at http://www.atomicmuseum.com/tour/sc2.cfm.
- Learn some chemistry basics at http://www.chem4kids.com.
- Find more chemistry basics at http://library.thinkquest.org/J001539.

☼ Find links to all kinds of kid-friendly games and activities at http://chemistry.about.com/od/chemistryforkids.
☼ Visit the National Atomic Museum at http://www
.atomicmuseum.com/tour/sc2.cfm.

 **AT THE LIBRARY**

CHEMISTRY LAB

Find ideas for all kinds of fun chemistry experiments in books such as:

Gardner, Robert, and Barbara Gardner Conklin. *Chemistry Science Fair Projects Using French Fries, Gumdrops, Soup, and Other Organic Stuff.* Berkeley Heights, N.J.: Enslow Publishers, 2004.

Hirschmann, Kris, and Deena Fleming. *Icky, Sticky, Foamy, Slimy, Ooey, Gooey Chemistry.* New York: Scholastic, 2006.

Loeschnig, Louis V. *No Sweat Science: Chemistry Experiments.* New York: Sterling, 2005.

Rhatigan, Joe, and Veronika Gunter. *Cool Chemistry Concoctions: 50 Formulas that Fizz, Foam, Splatter, and Ooze.* Asheville, N.C.: Lark Books, 2005.

CHEMICAL REACTIONS

Read about famous chemists and expand your scientific horizons with books such as:

Cohen, Judith Love. *You Can Be a Woman Chemist.* Marina del Rey, Calif.: Cascade Pass, 2005.

Gow, Mary. *Robert Boyle: Pioneer of Experimental Chemistry.* Berkeley Heights, N.J.: Enslow Publishers, 2005.

Kahn, Jetty. *Women in Chemistry Careers.* Mankato, Minn.: Capstone Press, 1999.

Newmark, Ann, and Laura Buller. *Chemistry.* New York: DK Children, 2005.

Yount, Lisa. *Antoine LeVoisier: Founder of Modern Chemistry.* Berkeley Heights, N.J.: Enslow Publishers, 2001.

🗣️ WITH THE EXPERTS

American Association of Pharmaceutical Scientists
2107 Wilson Boulevard, Suite 700
Arlington, VA 22201-3091
http://www.aapspharmaceutica.com

American Chemical Society
Education Division
1155 16th Street NW
Washington, DC 20036-4801
http://www.acs.org

American Institute of Chemical Engineers
Three Park Avenue
New York, NY 10016-5991
http://www.aiche.org

National Agricultural Chemicals Association
1156 15th Street NW, Suite 400
Washington, DC 20005-1704

Society of Plastics Engineers
14 Fairfield Drive
PO Box 403
Brookfield, CT 06804-39111
http://www.4spe.org

GET ACQUAINTED

Ellen Molner, Perfumer

CAREER PATH

CHILDHOOD ASPIRATION: To be a "mommy" and a professional.

FIRST JOB: Lab technician for a perfume company.

CURRENT JOB: Perfumer.

HAVE DEGREE, WILL WORK

Molner graduated from college with a degree in biology only to find that biology jobs were few and far between. With her unusual mix of artsiness and scientific knowledge to her approach, she wasn't sure which way to go with her career.

As fate would have it, answering a help-wanted ad sealed her destiny. The ad read simply "seeking lab tech, high school OK, college even better." She ended up assisting a chief perfumer—making compounds of the perfumer's formula—and discovered a whole new world of "creative" science.

The perfumer she worked for soon noticed her talent and offered her the opportunity to apprentice under him.

THE NOSE KNOWS

Her first task as a perfumer was to "develop a nose"—trade talk for learning to identify some 3,000 to 4,000 raw materials with a sniff. You've either got it or you don't when it comes to an olfactory skill like this. Luckily, Molner had it and was on her way to a fascinating career in this unusual specialty.

As daunting as this initial process sounds, Molner says that after so many years in the business she is so familiar with various scents that she can smell them in her sleep!

A PERFUME IS BORN

It starts with an idea. Clients come with a profile of a product they would like to bring to market. The profile contains all kinds of demographic information about the intended user: how old they are, how much money they make, what kinds of food they like to eat, their education level, what they want to smell like, etc. Perfumers keep these personal preferences in mind to develop scents that appeal to a specific audience.

Trends in society also dictate the way perfumes are designed. For instance, fragrances in the 1980s tended to be "loud" and ostentatious, and they were made with complicated mixes. Fragrances for the 1990s reflected simple yet sophisticated tastes with subtle differences between products for males and females. Fragrance in the 2000s come from a variety of surprising sources, as is true for a new perfume

Molner helped create for Ralph Lauren. The fragrance, called Polo Black for men, is a blend of iced mango, Spanish sage, silver armoise and sandalwood, and timberol and tonka bean.

Social scientist is just one more hat that perfumers wear to make sure that their potions meet with consumer demand.

YOU WIN SOME AND YOU LOSE SOME
Molner describes her work as 99 percent perspiration and 1 percent satisfaction. It's a tough, competitive business, and you don't always win the job. It's a real thrill to walk into a store and see a product that you had a hand in developing.

THANK HEAVENS FOR COMPUTERS
Computers store ingredient lists and information used to check chemical combinations for toxicology and safety standards (there isn't much demand for combustible or poisonous cologne!). This technology makes the work of a perfumer much easier.

ADVICE FOR YOUNG CHEMISTS
Molner heartily endorses a career in chemistry and says that there is always a need for serious scientists who can develop new chemistry. While jobs in the perfume industry are limited, there is plenty of room for chemists who can combine scientific process and creativity.

Engineer

WHAT IS AN ENGINEER?

Airplanes, oil fields, coal mines, automobile factories, skyscrapers—these are just a few of the places where you might find an engineer. Engineers are problem-solvers. They use the laws of math and science to figure out practical solutions to problems in many types of industries. Their job is to think up ways to use power and materials to make our world a better, safer, and more efficient place.

The oldest and most commonly known type of engineer is the civil engineer. These engineers design and guide the construction of structures such as buildings, roads, tunnels, bridges, and water systems. They also help reduce air pollution, improve transportation systems, and purify drinking water.

Other types of engineering specialists include the following:

Aerospace engineers work with aircraft, missiles and spacecraft.

Chemical engineers make new and better products from chemicals like rubber and petroleum. They create products like detergents, medicines, and plastics.

Electrical engineers harness electrical energy to operate things such as automobiles, computers, televisions, and missile guidance systems.

Industrial engineers work with people, machines, energy, and materials to figure out the best way to do a certain task. Their job is to find ways to get more out of less.

Manufacturing engineers start with 200 basic manufacturing processes and more than 40,000 materials to develop new processes for making products that range in sophistication from a jet fighter to a tube of lipstick.

Mechanical engineers work on two kinds of machines—either those that produce power like rocket engines or machines that use power like refrigerators.

Metallurgical engineers work to develop methods to process and convert metals into usable forms.

Mining engineers find, extract, and prepare minerals such as coal and copper for manufacturing use.

Nuclear engineers conduct research on the use of nuclear energy and radiation to generate electricity or for medical purposes.

Petroleum engineers explore and drill for oil and gas.

And still other specialties include automotive; agricultural; architectural; ceramic; computer; environmental; fire protection; geological; geothermal; heating, ventilation, and refrigeration; materials; naval; ocean; plastics; robotics and automated systems; safety; software; and transportation engineering.

Needless to say, with a list that long, engineering is a big field full of exciting opportunities. It's a demanding field but very rewarding both in terms of income potential and job satisfaction. Engineers are in demand in industry, business, government, research, teaching, and the military.

Most engineering jobs require at least a bachelor's degree, and many engineers go on to obtain a master's degree while they are working. Another way into the field is as an engineering technician, which requires only a degree from a two-year program.

So, what are you going to do when you grow up? How does designing a system to colonize the moon grab you? What about developing new laser technology that will save lives? And there's always the possibility of developing clean, efficient fuels out of garbage. Whatever you do as an engineer, you are sure to be on the cutting edge of technology and will help shape the next century.

☞ TRY IT OUT

BRIDGES 'R US

Here's your chance to build a bridge—virtually, of course. Just go online to the West Point Bridge Design Contest Web site at http://bridgecontest.usma.edu. There you can download free software that you can use to design a bridge. You can even test your idea to see if it passes a simulated load test.

Think your idea is ready for the real thing? If you are already 13 years old, you could be eligible to submit your idea in a national contest with scholarships and prizes and everything! See the Web site for details!

 **CHECK IT OUT**

 ON THE WEB

ONLINE ENGINEERING HOT SPOTS

Cruise down the information highway for some engineering know-how:

- ☀ Celebrate Engineers Week with ideas and resources from http://eweek.org
- ☀ Discover engineering at http://www.discoverengineering. org/home.asp
- ☀ Get Smarter at http://www.getsmarter.org
- ☀ Get Tech at http://www.gettech.org
- ☀ Explore engineering at http://www.engineeringk12 .org

PUT YOUR SKILLS TO THE TEST

Science contests and competitions provide a great way to stretch your engineering muscle. Here a few to explore:

- ☀ Junior Engineering Technical Society (JETS) at http:// www.jets.org
- ☀ MathCounts at http://www.mathcounts.org
- ☀ Odyssey of the Mind at http://www.odysseyofthe mind.com
- ☀ Science Olympiad at http://www.soinc.org

AT THE LIBRARY

HIT THE BOOKS

Go to the library and ask the librarian to help you find books about the particular type of engineering that you are most interested in. While you are there, see what kinds of information you can find about some of the most spectacular engineering feats that the world has ever seen: the Panama Canal, the Golden Gate Bridge, and shuttle spacecraft.

The three books below are full of challenging projects for the budding engineer. Check them out of your local library. If your library doesn't have a copy, ask your librarian to order one.

Adams, Richard Craig. *Engineering Projects for Young Scientists*. Revised ed. Danbury, Conn.: Franklin Watts, 2003.

Haslam, Andrew. *Building: Make It Work Science*. Minneapolis, Minn.: Two-Can Publishing, 2000.

Johmann, Carol A. *Bridges: Amazing Structures to Design, Build and Test*. Nashville, Tenn.: Williamson, 1999.

ENGINEERING MAGIC

How do they do that? Find out the secrets behind some of the engineering wonders of the world in this series of books:

Mann, Elizabeth. *Wonders of the World: Brooklyn Bridge*. New York: Mikaya Press, 2006.

———. *Wonders of the World: Empire State Building*. New York: Mikaya Press, 2006.

———. *Wonders of the World: Great Pyramids*. New York: Mikaya Press, 2006.

———. *Wonders of the World: Great Wall*. New York: Mikaya Press, 2006.

———. *Wonders of the World: Hoover Dam*. New York: Mikaya Press, 2006.

———. *Wonders of the World: Panama Canal*. New York: Mikaya Press, 2006.

WITH THE EXPERTS

American Engineering Association
4116 South Carrier Parkway, Suite 280
Grand Prairie, TX 75052-3200
http://www.aea.org

American Society for Engineering Education
1818 N Street NW, Suite 600
Washington, DC 20036-2479
http://www.asee.org

Junior Engineering Technical Society (JETS)
1420 King Street, Suite 405
Alexandria, VA 22314-2750
http://www.jets.org

Society for Women Engineers
230 East Ohio Street, Suite 400
Chicago, IL 60611-3265
http://www.swe.org

GET ACQUAINTED

Rose Lindsey, Industrial Engineer

CAREER PATH

CHILDHOOD ASPIRATION: Wasn't sure but noticed that she really liked math classes— especially solving problems, getting the answer "X = ," and underlining it twice!

FIRST JOB: Industrial engineer at the Charleston Naval Supply Yard in Charleston, South Carolina.

CURRENT JOB: Safety engineer at NASA's Marshall Space Flight Center in Huntsville, Alabama.

For 19 years, Rose worked with a payload operations control center (POCC) cadre of 15 to 20 people who support scientists and engineers from around the world when they conduct experiments onboard NASA's shuttle spacelab missions and the international space station. She recalls that one of the best parts of this job was the opportunity to work with many interesting scientists from places such as Canada, Europe, Japan, and Russia. Although Lindsey's work kept her earthbound (only the experiments she coordinated went to outer space), she was pleased that her work took her to Russia on several occasions.

A NEW BREED OF SPACECRAFT

Lindsey recently made a big career move and is now working with the Safety and Assurance team supporting the efforts of those responsible for developing a new crew exploration vehicle that "will carry NASA's future explorers to the moon, Mars, and beyond." The current space shuttles will be retired in 2010, and NASA is working to replace them with new systems that make the most of 21st century technology and ingenuity.

NASA learned some very hard lessons from the Challenger and Columbia disasters when both the crews and the spaceships were lost in horrible explosions. This makes the work of Lindsey's team especially important. Their job is to think through every possible thing that could go wrong with the new shuttle. They use a process called integrated hazard analysis to build "fault trees" where they identify potential problems and send their suggestions to systems engineers who test and analyze potential solutions.

It's probably hard to imagine the enormity of this task. They must examine every process and every piece of equipment to discover any potential catastrophes *before* the human crew and the very expensive spacecraft head into outer space in 2012. You can find out more about this exciting NASA project online at http://www.nasa.gov/missions/highlight/index.html.

BIGGEST SURPRISE ON THE JOB

Even though Lindsey's technical background in engineering is vital to her work with scientists and astronauts, Lindsey was surprised to learn that her writing and speaking skills were just as important. Working with so many different types of people from diverse cultures poses a continual challenge to Lindsey's communication and diplomatic abilities!

Lindsey has also discovered that it helps to unwind doing something totally different from the very technical work she does at NASA, which explains her two after-hours hobbies. She lets her imagination run free writing alternative country music, and she relaxes on weekends raising cattle on her family's farm in northern Alabama.

LINDSEY'S ADVICE TO FUTURE ENGINEERS

Find something that you love to do and a place where you can contribute something you believe in. Gain a solid engineering background that you can build on. Also, take advantage of any summer internships or cooperative education programs your school sponsors to get a firsthand look at engineering careers.

Food Scientist

WHAT IS A FOOD SCIENTIST?

As long as people need to eat, there will be opportunities in the food industry. If you've ever seen how much food a middle school football team can consume in one meal, it won't surprise you to learn that food is the world's largest industry. Billions of people depend on food scientists to find ways to feed the world efficiently and economically. With worldwide goals, it's no wonder that the field of food science is ripe with opportunity.

Food scientists use chemistry, microbiology, engineering, and other basic and applied sciences to find ways to produce, process, present, evaluate, and distribute food. Their work can be as diverse as managing a food firm, conducting research to improve flavor and shelf life, inspecting foods as part of a quality control process, or designing new packaging techniques. Food scientists are behind developments such as juice-in-a-box, fun fruits, and all those newfangled foods you find at fast-food restaurants.

Following are quick descriptions of some of the main specialties of this field:

Food processing involves converting raw foods into beverages, cereals, dairy products, meat and seafood products, fruit and vegetable products, snacks and convenience foods, and foods for animals.

Food research often means working in labs, test kitchens, and on production lines. Food researchers look for ways to improve the nutritional value, purity, taste, appearance, shelf life, convenience, and safety of foods while reducing their cost. They also work on developing new foods and finding solutions to the world's food problems.

Food biotechnology is a cutting-edge area. In a quest to improve crop production and quality and to produce raw products that can be converted into nutritious foods, some food scientists work with the highly specialized processes of plant breeding, gene splicing, microbial fermentation, and tissue cultures.

Food manufacturing involves building brand new foods from unusual sources.

Variety, opportunity, challenge: The field of food science has them waiting for a new generation of scientists. Think about these few food science problems waiting for you to solve:

- ☼ finding ways to turn low-cost food sources like soybeans, grains, and fishmeal into edible munchies

- developing foods for the first moon colony
- making broccoli and brussels sprouts as appealing to children as candy bars are
- improving methods for harvesting foods to expand the world's food supply
- inventing cool new snack foods for the kids of tomorrow

 TRY IT OUT

THE CORN CONNECTION

Corn: It's yellow. It's crunchy. It's fun to eat straight off the cob. Yeah, so what?

It's also an ingredient in many of the foods you eat. Go through the kitchen cupboards, read the food labels and make a list of all the foods that contain some form of corn (starch, syrup, meal, etc.).

Use information you find at the following Web sites to find out why a corn is used as an ingredient in each product on your list. Is it used to sweeten the taste? As a thickening agent? Add the corn's purpose next to the name of each product on your list.

- http://www.campsilos.org/mod3/students/c_history5. shtml
- http://www.ontariocorn.org/classroom/products. html
- http://www.iowacorn.org/cornuse/cornuse_3.html

Add to the fun with a visit to a virtual corn field online at http://www.iowafarmertoday.com/corn_cam and watch the corn grow over time.

PLAY WITH YOUR FOOD

The Institute of Food Technologists will send you a 32-page booklet with instructions for eight fairly easy food experiments. Request a copy from the address listed in Check It Out and have fun learning about the scientific principles of food.

✔ CHECK IT OUT

🖱 ON THE WEB
GO TO CYBER SCHOOL

Learn all you need to know to decide if a future in food science is the right choice for you. Do this by taking a complete minicourse on the food industry—compliments of the World Wide Web.

Introduction to the Food Industry is a self-study learning tool designed to help students explore the food industry and its career opportunities. You can link up to this self-taught and self-paced course at http://www.ift.org/cms/?pid=1000411.

Eight interesting and interactive lessons will guide you through food safety and quality assurance, food processing (how do you make peanut butter anyway?), nutrition, labeling and packaging, integrated resource management, distributing food from plant to store, marketing foods to shoppers, providing customer service, and preparing foods at home. Its lessons include learning objectives, a subject overview, career information, activities, questions, and lists of additional resources.

If you have even a teeny, tiny interest in this field, check out this Institute of Food Technologists Web site!

A WEB SITE BUFFET

A virtual smorgasbord of information about food science is available online at Web sites such as:

- Name that candy bar at http://www.sci.mus.mn.us/sln/tf/c/crosssection/namethatbar.html.
- Pop into some popcorn experiments at http://www.popweaver.com/popcorn101/science/science_list.html.
- Climb the food pyramid at http://www.mypyramid.gov/kids/kids_game.html.
- Study up on school meals at http://healthymeals.nal.usda.gov.
- http://www.foodscience.psu.edu/outreach/fun_food_science.html links to info on food and nutrition.

☙ Find answers to the question "what is food science" at
http://www.foodscience.psu.edu/Explore/explore.html.
☙ Get the latest news on the science of food at http://
psufoodscience.typepad.com.

 AT THE LIBRARY
WORLDWIDE DINNER
What's for dinner—around the world? Find out for yourself in
books such as:

Hollyer, Beatrice. *Let's Eat: What Children Eat Around the
World.* New York: Henry Holt, 2004.
Menzel, Peter and Faith D'Alusio. *Hungry Planet: What the
World Eats.* Berkeley, Calif.: Ten Speed, 2005.

Another fun source of global food information is the *Taste
of Culture* series published by KidHaven Press (Farmington
Hills, Mich.). The series features titles for China, France,
Germany, Greece, India, Iran, Italy, Japan, Mexico, Philippines,
Russia, Thailand, and Vietnam.

A MENU OF BOOKS
When it comes to food, the following books provide a smid-
gen of information and a sprinkling of inspiration for future
food scientists:

Allred, Alexandra Powe. *Nutrition.* Des Moines, Iowa: Perfec-
tion Learning, 2005.
Chelsea Clubhouse. *Food.* New York: Ferguson Publishing
Company, 2005.
Goodman, Susan E. *All in Just One Cookie.* New York: Green-
willow, 2006.
Green, Jen. *Genetically Modified Food.* Stargazer Books, 2005.
Schlosser, Eric and Charles Wilson. *Chew on This: Everything
You Don't Want to Know About Fast Food.* New York:
Houghton Mifflin, 2006.
Twist, Clint. *The Search for Food Breakthroughs.* Milwaukee,
Wisc.: Gareth Stevens Publishing, 2005.

👤≪ WITH THE EXPERTS

American Council on Science and Health
1995 Broadway, Second Floor
New York, NY 10023-5860
http://www.acsh.org

Institute of Food Technologists
525 West Van Buren, Suite 1000
Chicago, IL 60607-3823
http://www.ift.org/cms

National Agricultural Library
Abraham Lincoln Building
10301 Baltimore Avenue
Beltsville, MD 20705-2351
http://www.nal.usda.gov

Society for Nutrition Education
7150 Winton Drive, Suite 300
Indianapolis, IN 46268-4398
http://www.sne.org

GET ACQUAINTED

Roger Townley,
Food Scientist

CAREER PATH

CHILDHOOD ASPIRATION: To do something with food.

FIRST JOB: Sold produce from his family's garden door-to-door when he was in elementary school.

CURRENT JOB: Food scientist and owner of consulting company Townley Associates.

It all started with instant pudding, according to food scientist Roger Townley. When he was just a little kid, he liked to hang out with his mom in the kitchen, where she would let him "help out" by making simple things like that. But when he thinks back, he says that he was destined for a career in food. He recalls checking out cookbooks in the school library when he was in the third grade. Yes, he found the recipes interesting. But what he most liked to do was think about what he could do to change them. Now he realizes that, even then, it was clear he was headed for a career in food *science*, not as a chef or baker.

A LIFELONG PASSION FOR FOOD
Townley admits that he's a lucky guy to have found a way to blend his avocation (hobby) with his vocation (job). With over 30 year's of experience, he got his start with a college degree in bakery science. At first, he worked with a big national bakery company working with cookies, crackers, biscuits, PopTarts, and other "chemically leavened" baked goods. Although this provided a great start to his career, he eventually decided to broaden his horizons and enrolled in the food science program at North Carolina State University (which he says has one of the top five food science programs in the country) and earned a master's degree. From there he worked with all kinds of foods in a variety of companies before setting up his own consulting firm, Townley Associates. Now he provides product development and related technical services for food retailers and the restaurant industry.

WHO'S WHO IN FOOD
Take a look at Townley's Web site at http://pages.prodigy .net/townfam, and you'll find that his company has worked with some of the biggest food manufacturers in the country such as Sara Lee, Nabisco, Nestle, and Tyson. They also work with lots of restaurants. Ever heard of Boston Market, Dominos Pizza, Golden Corral, Pizza Hut, Red Lobster, Subway, and Taco Bell? Townley's team has worked with them all to develop good foods for people like you to enjoy.

One of his big clients is the North Carolina Sweet Potato Commission (http://www.ncsweetpotatoes.com). Once upon a time, the only occasion most people found for serving sweet potatoes was in holiday casseroles. Townley has helped the commission come up with more than 60 ways for people to use this very nutritious vegetable. He says not only did they find new recipes and ways to serve sweet potatoes (such as bagging them fresh cut, ready-made like carrots), but they also came up with new ways to use sweet potatoes as an ingredient in other products. For instance, did you know that sweet potatoes are an excellent fat replacement and can be used to replace up to 50 percent of the dairy ingredients in cream cheese and other types of cheeses. Townley says that not only do these substitutions add nutritional value; they also decrease the cost of producing dairy-rich products. It's the ultimate win-win that many of his clients are looking for.

IS IT A LAB OR IS IT A KITCHEN?

Townley cooks up formulas for new products in a facility that is part kitchen and part science lab. All the familiar fixtures of home are there—stove, refrigerator, and sink. But there are also some sophisticated meters, scales, and other scientific gadgets that help him develop prototypes for new food products.

Unlike the recipes you find in cookbooks that call for a cup of this and a tablespoon of that, Townley's formulas are based on formulas that call for 5 percent of one ingredient, 12 percent of another, and so on. That way, his clients can use the formulas to prepare as much or as little of a product as they need.

COOKING UP SOME CLUES FOR YOUR FUTURE

Townley has two recipes for your success. One is to make sure that you find something to do that you are really passionate about. He says that if you really enjoy your work, it will help you overcome just about any obstacle.

The second recipe is this: Don't be afraid to fail. There are hundreds (sometimes thousands) of flops behind every successful new product. Failure is a necessary part of success as a scientist. The good news is that, if you play your cards right, you'll catch your flops before they get to your clients!

Horticulturist

SHORTCUTS

GO take a hike, camp out overnight—anything that gets you outdoors, surrounded by nature.

READ Farmer's Almanac for some down-to-earth insight into growing things.

TRY growing plants from seeds—in a garden, homemade greenhouse, or window box.

WHAT IS A HORTICULTURIST?

Horticulture is an applied plant science. It combines art and science in the production, marketing, use, and improvement of fruits, vegetables, flowers, and ornamental plants. Horticulture is often a hobby (sometimes closer to an addiction) that's practiced in backyard gardens everywhere. People who actually make their living in horticulture are the envy of millions of amateur gardeners around the world.

Some of the ways that horticulturists practice the profession are

- maintaining botanical gardens, arboretums, and public parks
- owning and/or operating a wholesale or retail source of flowers, fruit, vegetables, or plants (for example, a garden center, nursery, greenhouse, farmer's market, or flower shop)
- teaching at colleges and universities or working in cooperative extension programs
- providing consultation services in landscaping, pest management, and other horticultural disciplines
- conducting research and development activities for business in areas like plant breeding, biotechnology, tissue culture, and horticulture chemical product development

☀ applying the science of raising plants to the business of running a farm to help farmers make a profit (country agricultural extension offices, research foundations, private farms and nurseries, and seed companies are likely employers)

☀ working for government agencies as plant inspectors, lobbyists, urban tree specialists, and zoning inspectors

☀ serving internationally to help developing countries resolve agricultural problems through programs such as the Peace Corps

Ecological concerns have created more opportunities for horticulturists with an environmentalist's point of view. Called environmental horticulturists, these scientists develop environmentally friendly or "healthy agriculture" techniques. Finding ways to protect crops without using toxic chemicals (pesticides and herbicides) is a major goal of their work. Environmental horticulturists are most often employed by universities or by the U.S. Department of Agriculture (USDA).

Another interesting specialty is horticultural therapy, which involves using plants and horticultural activities to help people with disabilities. Horticultural therapy is practiced in almost 300 hospitals in the United States, and more than a dozen colleges and universities offer horticultural therapy training programs.

Horticulture is one of those rare (and for many people, wonderful) occupations that combine a way to make a living with a way of life. It's a career that can grow on you if you find the idea of teaming up with Mother Nature appealing.

☞ TRY IT OUT

WHO TURNED OUT THE LIGHTS?

Science quiz! What is photosynthesis?

a. Those little booths in the mall where you can get your picture taken for a dollar.
b. The process through which plants capture light and convert it to chemical energy (plant food).
c. A fancy name for a one-hour photo developing shop.

Put a smiley face on your paper if you picked B!

Try this simple experiment to see photosynthesis at work. Here's what you'll need:

black construction paper	scissors
1 houseplant	tape

1. Make two small envelopes with the black paper.
2. Completely cover two leaves with the paper envelopes and secure with tape.
3. Just for fun, cut the remaining black paper into shapes and tape the shapes onto a couple leaves.
4. Put the plant in a sunny spot and make sure you keep it watered as usual.
5. After a week, uncover the leaves.
6. Record the results in a notebook.
7. Consider the following list of questions and see if you can come up with answers:
   - How did the covered leaves respond to the lack of light?
   - What does that tell you about photosynthesis?

☼ What happened to the leaves covered with the shapes?

☼ How are the covered portions different from the uncovered ones?

NAME THAT FLOWER

Compile a horticulture scrapbook full of pictures and notes about as many different kinds of plants, flowers, and trees as you can find. Illustrate your scrapbook with pictures clipped from magazines and catalogs and find information about each plant at Web sites such as:

☼ The Plants Gallery at http://plants.usda.gov/ gallery.html

☼ Flowerbase at http://www.flowerbase.com

✔ CHECK IT OUT

🖰 ON THE WEB

HOW DOES YOUR WEB SITE GROW?

You'll find an incredible amount of useful information about horticulture online. Some places to start include the following:

☼ Grow your horticultural knowledge at http://aggie-horticulture.tamu.edu/kindergarden/index.html.

☼ Visit horticulture paradise at http://hortparadise.unl. edu and be sure to look for the information just for teachers and kids.

☼ Find links to all kinds of horticulture resources for kids at http://www.ces.ncsu.edu/depts/hort/consumer/ hortinternet/youth.html.

☼ Start your own garden with tips found at http://www .kidsgardening.com.

☼ Harvest more gardening goodies at http://www .mastergardenproducts.com/kidsgarden.

AT THE LIBRARY

DIG INTO SOME GOOD BOOKS

Find out more about trees, plants, flowers, and all things horticultural in these books:

Branigan, Carrie, and Richard Dunne. *All Kinds of Plants*. Lawrenceburg, Ind.: Creative Company, 2005.

———. *Flowers and Seeds*. Lawrenceburg, Ind.: Creative Company, 2005.

Burnie, David. *Tree*. New York: DK Publishing, 2005.

———. *Plant*. New York: DK Publishing, 2006

Farndon, John. *Roots*. Farmington Hills, Mich.: Blackbirch Press, 2006.

Halpern, Monica. *Venus Flytraps, Bladderworts and Other Wild and Amazing Plants*. New York: National Geographic, 2006.

Lang, Gail. *Horticulture*. New York: Chelsea House Publications, 2006.

Spilsbury, Louise, and Richard Spilsbury. *Green Plants from Roots to Leaves*. Chicago: Heinemann, 2005.

———. *Why Do Plants Have Flowers?* Chicago: Heinemann, 2005.

WITH THE EXPERTS

American Horticultural Society
7931 East Boulevard Drive
Alexandria, VA 22308-1307
http://www.ahs.org

American Horticultural Therapy Association
201 East Main Street, Suite 1405
Lexington, KY 40507-2004
http://www.ahta.org

American Society for Horticultural Science
113 South West Street, Suite 200
Alexandria, VA 22314-2851
http://www.ashs.org

National Junior Horticultural Association
15 Railroad Avenue
Homer City, PA 15748-1378
http://www.njha.org

GET ACQUAINTED

Julius Nuccio, Horticulturist

IT'S ALL IN THE FAMILY

Julius Nuccio is part of the second gen-eration of family running this Califor-nia firm started by his father and uncle over 70 years ago. The Nuccios spe-cialize in growing camellias and azaleas and are renowned for cultivating some breathtak-ing varieties. Their flowers are grown outdoors year-round on a 10-acre farm and shipped to buyers all over the world.

CAREER PATH

CHILDHOOD ASPIRATION: Any-thing but work at his father's nursery.

FIRST JOB: Besides helping with the flowers at the nursery, working in a gas station.

CURRENT JOB: Co-owner of Nuc-cio Nurseries, growers of world-class camellias and azaleas.

GO TO COLLEGE OR GET TO WORK!

After Nuccio graduated from high school, his father gave him a choice of going to college or getting to work. He didn't like the idea of spending more time in school and had decided that he didn't want to spend the rest of his life pumping gas, so he chose to work at the nursery until he figured out some-thing better to do.

He didn't realize then how much he enjoyed working outdoors, being his own boss, and playing with nature. Now, several decades later, Nuccio says he has no regrets over his decision.

73

APPRENTICE TO THE BEST
Unlike many horticulturists, Nuccio has no formal training in the profession. Instead, he learned from the two best teachers in the world—his father and uncle. After years of on-the-job training and a desire to learn something new every day, Nuccio can boast a nursery with the reputation of one of the finest camellia growers in the country.

THE BIRDS AND THE BEES
You'd be amazed to discover how many different kinds of camellias and azaleas there are. That's because horticulturists like Nuccio constantly work to add new specimens to the family by crossbreeding them. By mixing two kinds of flowers, these flower scientists cultivate new species that can differ in color and shape as well as growth habits. For instance, camellias were once only grown in warmer regions of the country. Crossbreeding has resulted in the creation of hardier hybrids that can withstand colder temperatures.

Crossbreeding isn't a quick process. It can take five to seven years from the beginning of the process until there is enough stock built up to take to market. While a horticulturist may graft anywhere from 5 to 50,000 seedlings to start the process, it is quite common for only 3 to 10 samples to survive. The cutting and grafting procedure continues until there are enough samples to get a good picture of the new species. A new species is officially born when nature takes over and the birds and the bees start pollinating.

IT GROWS ON YOU
When Nuccio was a teenager, he never expected to be doing what he's doing now and enjoying it so much. Over the years he has found a great deal of satisfaction in his work. He says that horticulture is not a way to get rich quick but that it's a great way to enjoy earning a good living. He encourages anyone with an interest in working with plants to combine learning from books with gaining hands-on experience.

Landscape Architect

WHAT IS A LANDSCAPE ARCHITECT?

Close your eyes and imagine your favorite outdoor place. Is it a park? Near the seashore? Your own backyard? Chances are that a landscape architect had a hand in designing some of the beautiful outdoor places you see everyday.

One of the first, and most enduring, examples of landscape architecture in the United States was the design of New York City's Central Park. Two men, Frederick Law Olmsted and Calvert Vaux, combined their talents to create a green oasis of quiet in the middle of a bustling, concrete city.

In simple terms, the goal of a landscape architect is to beautify the places where people live and work. You've seen their handiwork in places like parks, malls, college campuses, corporate sites, cemeteries, resorts, and residential developments. Landscape architects design these areas so that they are functional and compatible with the natural environment.

An emerging specialty within the field is the environmental landscape architect. With an eye toward environmental responsibility and stewardship of the land, environmental landscape architects design, plan, modify, and enhance large tracts of land. Some ecologically conscious projects involve restoring wetlands and woodlands to their natural habitat—sometimes re-creating entire ecosystems with the indigenous (native) plants, animals, and birds that once thrived on a particular site. Other projects actually turn garbage dumps into parks.

Another interesting specialty is historic preservation. This work combines a love of history and gardening with design. In order to re-create historically accurate surroundings for historic sites and landmarks, historic preservation landscape architects must dig for details about how people lived and what they grew during a specific time and place in history.

Computers, computer-aided design (CAD) tools, and video simulation equipment are used by all kinds of landscape architects to design livable environments and make detailed plans. They work with teams of urban planners, landscapers, and contractors to implement the plans.

Today's landscape architects must have a strong background in science and be well versed in the areas of ecology, botany, and biology. All this is incorporated into a knowledge of design, construction, plants, and soils. A strenuous testing and licensing process weeds out the unprepared.

Landscape architecture is an appealing profession for those who like to learn on their own, love working outdoors, and don't mind getting their hands dirty.

☞ TRY IT OUT

MY FIRST GARDEN

Gather stacks of magazines and gardening catalogs and cut out pictures of the flowers and gardens that you like best. Arrange these pictures on a large sheet of poster board to sketch out plans for a beautiful garden that you'd like to grow someday.

GARDEN DETECTIVE

Start noticing the gardens in your communities in parks, people's yards, botanic gardens and wherever else you can find them. Every time you find one, make a quick sketch in a notebook of how the garden looks and jot down a list of the things you like best about each garden.

BRING YOUR OWN HOE

Link up with your local garden club or botanical garden. These groups can be a great source of education and hands-on learning opportunities. Take classes, go on tours, and volunteer to help with community gardening projects. Listen and learn from people who are madly in love with gardening. One place to look for gardening activities is your local 4-H Club. Go online to http://4husa.org to find a link to your state's 4-H Web site.

✔ CHECK IT OUT

🖰 ON THE WEB

GARDEN VARIETY WEB SITES

Go online to cultivate some landscaping ideas.

- ☼ Find tips for planting a garden at http://www.urbanext .uiuc.edu/firstgarden.
- ☼ Explore the history of landscaping at http://darkwing .uoregon.edu/~helphand.
- ☼ Plant some stuff with advice from Kid's Valley Garden at http://www.copper-tree.ca/garden/index.html.

- ☼ Experience gardening as both a science and an art at http://www.exploratorium.edu/gardening.
- ☼ Get a sneak peek at the secret life of flowers at http://www.exploratorium.edu/gardening/bloom/ secret_life_of_flowers.

 AT THE LIBRARY

GARDEN READING

Plant yourself in front of a good book about gardening such as:

Bull, Jane. *The Gardening Book*. New York: DK Publishing, 2003.

Chasek, Ruth. *Essential Gardening for Teens*. New York: Scholastic, 2000.

Claybourne, Anna. *Plant Secrets*. Chicago, Ill.: Raintree, 2005.

Lovejoy, Sharon. *Roots, Shoots, Buckets & Boots*. New York: Workman Publishing Group, 1999.

Krezel, Cindy. *Kid's Container Gardening: Year-Round Projects for Inside and Out*. Batavia, Ill.: Ball, 2005.

Markey, Kevin. *Secrets of Disney's Glorious Gardens*. New York: Disney Editions, 2006.

Stefoff, Rebecca. *The Flowering Plant Division*. New York: Benchmark Books, 2005.

🗣 WITH THE EXPERTS

American Society of Landscape Architects
636 Eye Street, NW
Washington, DC 20001-3736
http://www.asla.org

Professional Landcare Network
950 Herndon Parkway, Suite 450
Herndon, VA 20170-5531
http://www.landcarenetwork.org

Society for Ecological Restoration
285 West 18th Street, Suite 1
Tucson, AZ 85701-2563
http://www.ser.org

GET ACQUAINTED

Ben Page,
Landscape Architect

CAREER PATH

CHILDHOOD ASPIRATION:
To follow the family tradition of medical practice.

FIRST JOB: Working at a Dairy Queen for 90 cents an hour.

CURRENT JOB: Owner of a landscape architecture firm.

Ben Page had always planned on becoming a doctor. But, once at college, he discovered that he just wasn't cut out for that profession. His grades starting dropping, and he realized that he needed to come up with another plan fast. He started talking to people whose opinions he respected. One friend encouraged him to think about what he really liked doing.

It didn't take long to figure out that some of his happiest memories centered around his grandparents' farm. He loved being outdoors, was fascinated with design, and was really interested in ecologically based conservation.

Page put aside med school for a new focus: landscape architecture. He transferred to a new school and watched his grades go way up as he found a field of study that fit him better.

FROM THE SIMPLE TO THE EXTRAORDINARY

Page's work as a landscape architect can be as simple as determining the best type of shade tree to use in a client's yard or as complex as a five-year project restoring a 2,000-acre woodland and animal preserve with natural prairie,

marsh, and meadow and an ecologically appropriate food chain. This latter project involved extensive research into things like native grasses, 19th-century plowing techniques, and appropriate food sources for red-tailed hawks.

Page designs beautiful environments for people's homes as well as corporate sites. He has even developed a master plan for the vice president's gardens in Washington, D.C. From now on the vice president will be greeting dignitaries and enjoying private family picnics in style. The formal garden is similar in scale to the Rose Garden at the White House. The private garden is designed to be a relaxing oasis for the nation's "second family."

A LITTLE SOMETHING FOR EVERYONE

One of the aspects about landscape architecture that Page finds most satisfying is that it offers a challenging way to combine personal interests and passions. For instance, while his personal bent is intensively focused on design, other landscape architects focus more on ecological or historic preservation aspects of the field. One noted colleague is well known for bizarre, surreal garden interpretations such as his bagel park. The history buffs in Page's field help complete pictures of how people used to live by re-creating historically accurate gardens and landscaping at national landmarks.

IT'S MORE THAN PLANTING TREES

According to Page, landscape architecture is a wonderful way to leave a lasting contribution to the quality of life for future generations. He views the field as an exceptionally rewarding alternative to some of the more traditional science- and math-oriented professions. It's a profession with a positive job outlook—he'd like to see more bright young people consider it.

Medical Technologist

WHAT IS A MEDICAL TECHNOLOGIST?

What happens to the blood sample you give at the doctor's office or the little cup you fill in the doctor's bathroom? They go to a laboratory for medical technologists to test. These medical detectives test blood, urine, body fluids, and tissues to find clues of diseases and other health problems. Doctors and other medical professionals depend on accurate lab work to diagnose and treat many serious illnesses such as AIDS, diabetes, and cancer. Vital test results may often mean a matter of life or death; accuracy is a critical part of this work.

Depending on the size and scope of the lab itself, medical technologists typically work in one or more of five areas in the laboratory, namely

blood banks, where technologists are responsible for drawing donor blood, separating blood into its components, and identifying and matching components to ensure safe transfusions.

chemistry, where technologists analyze the chemical composition of blood and body fluids.

hematology, where technologists count, describe, and identify cells in blood and other body fluids (this information helps detect diseases like anemia and leukemia).

immunology, where technologists study biological defenses against viruses or allergy-causing agents.

microbiology, where technologists look for microorganisms such as bacteria, parasites, and fungi.

Tools used in the medical laboratory include microscopes, complex electronic equipment, computers, and other precision instruments, some of which can cost millions of dollars.

To become a medical technologist you'll need to earn a four-year college degree. One particularly interesting option for those pursuing a career as a medical technologist is to work part time in a medical lab as a medical lab technician while studying to become a technologist. The minimum requirements for a technician can be a high school diploma with some specialized training.

A medical laboratory technician performs general tests working under the direct supervision of a technologist. He or she hunts for clues to the absence, presence, extent, and causes of disease. It can be a rewarding career in and of itself or as a stepping stone to higher levels of responsibility.

A medical lab technician is a step below a medical technologist in training and responsibility; a pathologist is a step above a technologist. Pathologists are fully trained and accredited medical doctors who specialize in providing and interpreting laboratory information to help diagnose health problems and to monitor the progress of treatment.

Pathologist might be another option to consider in a long-term career plan.

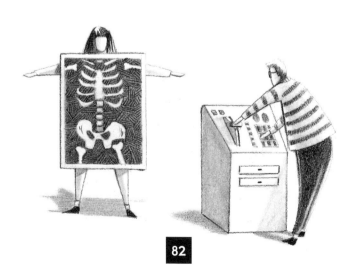

 TRY IT OUT

FOLLOW THAT BLOOD SAMPLE!

Using information you find on the Internet, resources you dig up from the library, and any helpful advice you can get from professionals, make a chart tracing the path of a typical blood sample from the time it leaves the patient's body to the time the results arrive back at the doctor's office.

You'll find useful resources at htp://www.labtestonline.org/lab/samples.html. Make a chart illustrating the process.

GET IN THE HABIT OF SAVING LIVES

Call the local branch of the American Heart Association or the American Red Cross and find out about the cardiopulmonary resuscitation (CPR) and/or first aid courses that they offer. Although these skills are not part of the lab tech's job description, they'll give you a good introduction to medical practices and the lifesaving importance of following very specific procedures. Good preparation for anyone entering the medical field.

Go online to http://www.redcross.org to find out about local Red Cross activities.

✔ CHECK IT OUT

🖱 ON THE WEB

MEDICAL MAYHEM ONLINE

Have fun playing around at some of the scientific Web sites:

- Visit a virtual medical technology lab at http://www.knowitall.org/kidswork/hospital/realpeople/people/lab.html.
- Explore biology, the science behind medical technology, at http://www.hhmi.org/coolscience.
- Discover the hidden world of microbes at the Microbe Zoo at http://commtechlab.msu.edu/sites/dlc-me/zoo/index.html.

- ☼ Tour the Exploratorium's "Revealing Bodies" exhibit online at http://www.exploratorium.edu/bodies.
- ☼ Check out the Center for Disease Control and Prevention's kid's page at http://www.cdc.gov/gcc/exhibit/kids.htm.

DNA AND Y-O-U

Get up close and personal with deoxyribonucleic acid. Better known as DNA, it's the stuff that makes you *you*.

- ☼ First stop is the American Museum of Natural Science Web site at http://www.ology.amnh.org/genetics.
- ☼ Discover the secret of photo 51 at http://www.pbs.org/wgbh/nova/photo51.
- ☼ Find out about DNA was discovered at http://www.dnaftb.org/dnaftb.
- ☼ Learn about DNA and play some gene games at http://www.genecrc.org/site/ko/index_ko.htm.

AT THE LIBRARY

THE READING LAB

Investigate the world of medicine in books such as:

Brown, Jeremy. *Four-Minute Forensic Mysteries: Shadow of Doubt.* New York: Scholastic Paperbacks, 2006.

Libal, Angela. *Fingerprints, Bite Marks, Ear Prints: Human Signposts.* Broomall, Pa.: Mason Crest Publishers, 2005.

Rainis, Kenneth G. *Blood and DNA Evidence: Crime-Solving Science Experiments.* Berkeley Heights, N.J.: Enslow Publishers, 2006.

Routh, Kristina. *Medicine.* Mankato Minn.: Smart Apple Media, 2005.

Woog, Adam. *The Microscope.* Farmington Hills, Mich.: Lucent Books, 2003.

WITH THE EXPERTS

American Society of Clinical Pathologists
33 West Monroe, Suite 1600
Chicago, IL 60603-5308
http://www.ascp.org

Intersociety Committee on Pathology Information
9650 Rockville Pike
Bethseda, MD 20814-3999

National Accrediting Agency for Clinical Laboratory Sciences
8410 West Bryn Mawr Avenue, Suite 670
Chicago, IL 60631-3408
http://www.naacls.org

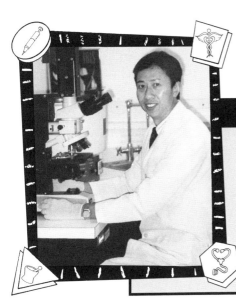

GET ACQUAINTED

Henry C. Lee,
Medical Technologist

CAREER PATH

CHILDHOOD ASPIRATION:
To become a doctor.

FIRST JOB: Research assistant
in a genetics laboratory.

CURRENT JOB: Technical
support specialist at a firm
that produces instruments
for clinical labs.

Henry C. Lee has been a medical technologist for almost 20 years. He started out in a lab working as a bench technologist. That's someone who actually draws samples and conducts tests. After that, he worked in a university hospital specializing in the chemistry side of things—solving problems and developing new tests. A favorite part of the job for him was the opportunity to teach nearby university students about medical technology. He spent several years as a supervisor in a large clinical lab before switching over to work in a medical equipment corporation.

Lee's new job is a big change from what he's done in the past. The focus is on training lab staff to use sophisticated testing equipment and on trouble-shooting problems with instruments.

WHEN ALL ELSE FAILS, GO TO PLAN B

When Lee started college he had every intention of going on to medical school to become a doctor. However, he made the mistake of spending too much time at the beach and not enough time hitting the books. After the first two years, he realized his grades weren't high enough to get accepted into med school, so he started looking at other options.

He sought the advice of friends and relatives and eventually decided that becoming a medical technologist was a good alternative. After earning a bachelor's degree in microbiology, Lee went through the internship, training, and licensure requirements to become a fully certified medical technologist. It's been the key to an interesting and rewarding career in medicine.

MIND YOUR P'S AND Q'S

In a work environment where thousands of tests can be run every day, Lee says you have to learn to work efficiently and provide consistently correct results. There's a lot at stake when you are talking about a person's health and well-being. Tragic consequences can be the result of careless mistakes. Lee has learned to work like a detective gathering all the clues and tracking down the evidence to give doctors the most reliable results possible.

IF HE HAD TO DO IT ALL OVER AGAIN

He says he'd buckle down and study harder. When you're young, sometimes you don't quite understand how the decisions you make can affect the rest of your life. He learned the hard way how important it is to concentrate and stay focused on what you really want. Although it's easier to let spur-of-the-minute opportunities sway you, it's important to keep sight of the future.

Meteorologist

WHAT IS A METEOROLOGIST?

True or false? Most meteorologists report weather news on TV and radio shows. False. Around 90 percent of professional meteorologists are operational or research scientists who work behind the scenes to increase the accuracy of forecasts and weather warnings that affect human life. While weather reporting is an important function of meteorology, much work goes on away from the camera to prepare valid weather news.

The American Meteorologist Society defines meteorologist as a person with specialized education "who uses scientific principles to explain, understand, observe or forecast the earth's atmospheric phenomena and/or how the atmosphere [the air that covers the earth] affects the earth and life on the planet." The primary goal of meteorologists is to completely understand and accurately predict atmospheric phenomena or weather. Lives and livelihood depend on it.

Meteorologists study data on air pressure, temperature, humidity, and wind velocity to make their predictions. They apply physical and mathematical relationships to make short- and long-term weather forecasts. Sophisticated equipment and computer resources such as Doppler radar help make their work more exact. Since the weather business is a 24-hours-a-day, seven-days-a-week operation, someone is always on the watch.

While weather forecasting is one of the best-known applications of meteorology, there are other important applications as well. For instance, some meteorologists work to find ways to control air pollution, others specialize in fields such as agriculture, air and sea transportation, or defense, and still others study trends such as global warming.

Specialties within the field include

Operational meteorology: weather forecasting.

Physical meteorology: study of weather phenomena.

Climatology: analysis of past records of sunshine, wind, rainfall, and temperatures in specific areas.

Research meteorology: in-depth study of specific aspects of meteorology. Research meteorologists have made some important discoveries in the recent past. One of the most exciting and useful outcomes of recent meteorological

research was the development of an accurate, automatic wind-shear detection and warning system that is now used at major airports all over the United States to provide safer air travel. This safeguard was the direct result of the meteorological study of microbursts.

The National Oceanic and Atmospheric Administration is one of the largest employers of meteorologists. According to a survey conducted by the American Meteorological Society, private industry is a growing sector of employment for meteorologists, with about a third of all meteorologists working for businesses or television stations, a third working at colleges and in research positions, and another third working for the government.

☞ TRY IT OUT

WEATHER STATION
Go to the library and borrow a copy of *The Ben Franklin Book of Easy & Incredible Experiments, Activities, Projects and Science Fun* (A Franklin Institute of Science Museum Book, New York: John Wiley & Sons, Inc., 1995). It gives instructions for making six instruments that will help you observe and forecast the weather.

- thermometer
- barometer
- wind vane
- anemometer
- hygrometer
- rain gauge

Voilà! your own weather station. Use these six instruments to keep track of the weather in your own backyard.

WEATHER STATION
If you can't find a copy of this book, go online to find instructions at The Franklin Institute Online at http://sln.fi.edu/weather/todo/todo.html or the Miami Museum of Science Web site at http://www.miamisci.org/hurricane/weatherstation.html.

WEATHER-WATCHER

Make a big chart with space to record the weather forecast for your city for an entire week. Use information you find in the local newspaper and at the Weather Channel Online (http://www.weather.com) to list what the weather is expected to be each day. Update your chart each day with your personal observations of what the weather was really like. How often did the weather experts get it right?

✔ CHECK IT OUT

🖱 ON THE WEB

The Internet is a great source of information about all kinds of weather-related phenomenon, as you'll discover in these Web sites:

- ☼ Get weather wise at http://www.weatherwizkids.com.
- ☼ Find out what different weather instruments are used for at http://schoolscience.rice.edu/duker/winstruments.html.
- ☼ Explore careers in earth science at http://kids.earth.nasa.gov/archive/career/index.html.
- ☼ Find links to all kinds of information about meteorology at http://www.kidsolr.com/science/page14.html.
- ☼ Go wild for weather at http://www.wildwildweather.com.
- ☼ Hunt down some hurricanes at http://www.fema.gov/kids/hurr.htm.
- ☼ Tango with an online tornado at http://www.tornadoproject.com.
- ☼ Give yourself an online meteorology education at http://meted.ucar.edu/comm_k12.htm.

📚 AT THE LIBRARY

WEATHER READS

Read up on the weather in books such as:

Breen, Mark, and Kathleen Friestad. *The Kid's Book of Weather Forecasting*. Charlotte, Vt.: Williamson Publishing Company, 2003.

Challoner, Jack. *Eyewitness: Hurricane & Tornado*. New York: DK Children, 2004.

Cosgrove, Brian. *Eyewitness: Weather*. New York: DK Children, 2004.

Rodgers, Alan, and Angella Streluk. *Forecasting the Weather*. Chicago, Ill.: Heinemann, 2002.

Schley, William F. *Forecasting*. Des Moines, Iowa: Perfection Learning, 2004.

Wills, Susan, and Steven R. Wills. *Meteorology: Predicting the Weather*. Minneapolis: Oliver Press, 2003.

WITH THE EXPERTS

American Meteorological Society
45 Beacon Street
Boston, MA 02108-3693
http://www.ametsoc.org

Association of American Weather Observers
627 Als Welding Road
Spirit Lake, ID 83869-9661
http://www.aawo.net

Franklin Institute Science Museum
222 North 20th Street
Philadelphia, PA 19103-1115
http://www.fi.edu

Hurricane Research Division
Atlantic Oceanographic and Meteorological Laboratory
4301 Rickenbacker Causeway
Miami, FL 33149-1026
http://www.aoml.noaa.gov/hrd

National Climatic Data Center
Federal Building
151 Patton Avenue
Asheville, NC 28801-5001
http://www.ncdc.noaa.gov

National Severe Storms Laboratory
120 David L. Boren Boulevard
Norman, OK 73072-7303
http://www.nssl.noaa.gov

National Weather Service
1325 East West Highway
Silver Spring, MD 20910-3280
http://www.nws.noaa.gov

GET ACQUAINTED

John Morales, Meteorologist

CAREER PATH

CHILDHOOD ASPIRATION:
Something having to do with
the sky.

FIRST JOB: Handing out tools
to fix machines.

CURRENT JOB: Chief meteorologist for NBC-Telemundo in
Miami.

FOCUSED DETERMINATION

From the time he was a teenager, John Morales knew his life's
work would center around the sky. He considered becoming
a pilot or pursuing a career as an astronomer and finally set-
tled on becoming a meteorologist. With that goal in mind, he
went to the library to look up colleges that provided training
in meteorology. He chose Cornell and graduated in 1984.

HOME SWEET HOME

Raised in Puerto Rico, Morales had a job waiting for him there
when he graduated. He spent seven years working with the
National Weather Service in San Juan, Puerto Rico, Louisiana,
and Washington, D.C.

ONE OF A KIND

Morales was the first meteorologist in the United States broadcasting to a Spanish-speaking audience. As a fill-in meteorologist for the weekend edition of the *Today* show, Morales is also the first Latino meteorologist to broadcast to an English-language, national audience. There are other Hispanic weather reporters but only a handful with professional meteorology credentials. He's looking for some competition!

MOONLIGHTING

Morales is in demand! Along with broadcasting weather reports for four different television shows, he is frequently called to conduct research and provide expert testimony in a highly specialized area of meteorology called forensic meteorology. This involves determining how weather affected past events such as airplane crashes. He also does some weather-related consulting for businesses that need very detailed forecasts, such as ski resorts, agricultural companies, aviation companies, and radio stations.

CONGRATULATIONS!

Morales won a regional Emmy award for his work producing a news video in Spanish called *48 Hours Before the Storm: Step-by-Step Preparation for Hurricanes.* He had plenty of hands-on experience to prepare him for the task. This proved especially true during the 2004 and 2005 hurricane seasons when a total of eight hurricanes struck or brushed by the state of Florida.

BY THE WAY . . .

Remember that Morales said he had three interests in the sky? Well, to one degree or another, he's fulfilled goals in every area. He's an accomplished meteorologist, he earned his private pilot's license, and he studied some astronomy at Cornell University.

Nutritionist

SHORTCUTS

SKILL SET

✔ **BUSINESS**

✔ **SCIENCE**

✔ **TALKING**

GO pick one of your favorite recipes and figure out a way to reduce the fat or calories by substituting different ingredients. Serve it to your family or friends and find out what they think.

READ cookbooks, magazines that focus on healthy lifestyles (*Cooking Light* is a good one), and food trivia books.

TRY keeping a record of everything you eat for a week.

WHAT IS A NUTRITIONIST?

You are what you eat. No one understands the connection between good food and good living better than someone who specializes in the science of nutrition. The very nature of nutritionists' work requires them to be part junk food cop, part healthy food cheerleader. Their job is to prevent and treat diseases through good eating habits.

Another name for nutritionist is *dietitian*. You'll find dietitians working in many kinds of places, some expected, like hospitals and schools, and some unexpected, like professional sports associations and advertising agencies. The main professional specialties are the following:

Clinical dietitians work in hospitals, clinics, extended care facilities, or nursing homes. They are considered a vital part of the medical team as they develop and monitor nutritional plans to help patients recover from illnesses or to control serious diseases. Some dietitians specialize in a particular area such as nutrition for diabetics, heart patients, or pediatric patients.

Management dietitians work just about anywhere large quantities of food are served: schools, prisons, corporate

cafeterias, hotel and restaurant chains, and hospital food service systems. They are responsible for managing staff, planning menus, purchasing food supplies, and maintaining a budget.

Community dietitians help people improve the quality of their lives with proper nutrition. They counsel families, the elderly, pregnant women, children, people with disabilities, and underprivileged people. Community dietitians often augment the staff of child care facilities, government programs, and public health agencies.

Sports and fitness nutritionists are relatively new. These nutritionists work with professional athletes, sports teams, scholastic athlete teams, and individuals to determine the best diet to assure peak performance. In addition to working for professional teams or college and university athlete programs, sports nutritionists can also be employed by health and fitness clubs, gyms, and sports medicine clinics.

 # TRY IT OUT

CLIMB THE PYRAMID

The U.S. Department of Agriculture has gone to extreme measures to determine the perfect mix of foods for a healthy human diet. Their findings have been summed up in five basic food groups, called the food pyramid: grain, fruit, vegetable, milk, and meat and beans.

Go online to http://www.mypyramid.gov to find out more.

Then make a chart with five columns—one for each food group—and do the following exercises to get better acquainted with these food groups:

Beginner: Go through your kitchen cabinets, pantry, or refrigerator and list each food item that you find in the proper category.

Amateur: Keep track of the menus served at the school cafeteria for a week. List each food in the appropriate column to determine how well-balanced the meals are.

Expert: Tag along the next time your parent goes to the supermarket. Find five new foods (things you've never tasted before) for each category and write them in the correct column. Ask your parent if you can try one of your discoveries for dinner.

AN OUNCE OF PREVENTION IS WORTH A POUND OF CURE

Do a little research about some diet-related diseases. Diabetes, heart disease, and cancer are three of the major diseases on which diet has a great effect. Make a list of recommended foods for either preventing the disease or keeping it under control. Using your list of approved foods, plan a healthy menu for breakfast, lunch, and dinner.

Good places to look for information are organizations devoted to finding cures for these diseases. Check the local phone book for a local chapter of the following organizations:

- American Cancer Society (http://www.cancer.org)
- American Diabetes Association (http://www.diabetes.org)
- American Heart Association (http://www.americanheart.org)

SNACK FOOD MAKEOVER

Are you eating too much junk food? Make a list of your 10 favorite snacks. Put a star next to each snack food on your list that fits on the USDA Food Pyramid (see Climb the Pyramid activity above). For instance, if ice cream is on your list it would count as a milk and dairy food choice. Put an X over those items that would, in all honesty, be considered junk food or completely empty of any nutritional value whatsoever. Next to those items come up with an idea for another, more nutritious food that you'd enjoy munching. Could you trade in your crispy, high-calorie potato chips for whole wheat crackers or crunchy veggies?

✔ CHECK IT OUT

🖱 ON THE WEB

A MENU OF WEB SITES

Once again the Internet is the place to be for up-to-the-minute information about nutrition. See for yourself at these Web sites:

- Stop by the Nutrition Café at http://exhibits.pacsci.org/nutrition.
- Visit the Cool Food Planet at http://www.coolfoodplanet.org/gb/kidz.
- Play with your food at http://www.nutritionexplorations.org.
- Get off the couch and take the verb challenge at http://www.verbnow.com.

📚 AT THE LIBRARY

WORDS TO CHEW ON

Dig into some of these books about food and nutrition:

Allred, Alexandra Powe. *Nutrition.* Des Moines, Iowa: Perfection Learning, 2004.

Bueller, Laura. *Eyewitness: Food.* New York: DK Publishing, 2005.

D'Amico, Joan, and Karen Eich Drummond. *The Healthy Body Cookbook.* New York: John Wiley & Sons, 1999.

Douglas, Ann. *Body Talk: Straight Facts About Fitness, Nutrition, and Feeling Great About Yourself.* Toronto, Canada: Maple Tree Press, 2006.

Libal, Autumn. *The Importance of Physical Activity and Exercise.* Broomall, Pa.: Mason Crest Publishers, 2005.

Mason, Paul. *Training for the Top: Nutrition and Exercise.* Chicago: Raintree, 2005.

Sohn, Emily, and Sarah Webb. *Food and Nutrition.* New York: Chelsea Clubhouse, 2005.

🗣️ WITH THE EXPERTS

American Society for Nutrition
9650 Rockville Pike
Bethesda, MD 20814-3999
http://www.nutrition.org

American Dietetic Association
120 South Riverside Plaza, Suite 2000
Chicago, IL 60606-6995
http://www.eatright.org

Food and Nutrition Information Center
Agricultural Research Service, USDA
National Agricultural Library, Room 105
10301 Baltimore Avenue
Beltsville, MD 20705-2351
http://www.nal.usda.gov/fnic

National Association of Sports Nutrition
7710 Balboa Avenue, Suite 227B
San Diego, CA 92111-2261
http://www.nasnutrition.com

School Nutrition Association
700 South Washington Street, Suite 300
Alexandria, VA 22314-4252
http://www.schoolnutrition.org

GET ACQUAINTED

Leslie Bonci, Registered Dietitian

CAREER PATH

CHILDHOOD ASPIRATION: Linguist (someone who studies and speaks foreign languages).

FIRST JOB: Researcher for a cancer study about the effects of smoking.

CURRENT JOB: Nutritional consultant.

Leslie Bonci graduated from college with a degree in biopsychology but wasn't sure what to do with her career. She got hooked on the nutrition side of science when she took a nutrition class taught by an especially dynamic woman. The funny thing is her grandmother had told her she'd make a good nutritionist long before she even started considering the field.

FOOTBALL PLAYERS AND BALLERINAS

As part of her private practice, Bonci acts as nutritional consultant for the Pittsburgh Steelers, Pittsburgh Ballet Theater,

Pittsburgh Pirates, Pittsburgh Penguins, and the Toronto Blue Jays. Needless to say, these groups have very different nutritional needs.

She works with individuals helping them plan a diet that will get them to their ideal fighting or dancing weight. She shows them how to shop for food and gives them ideas for preparing food. She also works with the entire football team or corps de ballet, addressing nutrition concerns during training and arranging for appropriate food service when the groups travel. In addition, she works with all the sports teams at the University of Pittsburgh.

THE NUTRITION GAME

Somewhere along the line, sports nutrition became a special niche for Bonci. Her interest in sports nutrition comes naturally though. Bonci is a marathon runner who has discovered firsthand how eating habits help athletic performance. Therefore, motivating athletes to make healthy eating a part of their lifestyle is very important.

NO TIME FOR BOREDOM

As if all this didn't keep Bonci busy enough, she also works in a hospital setting. This work involves helping patients with nutrition-related diseases such as diabetes, colitis, and cancer use the right foods to help keep their medical problems under control. She takes a special interest in helping young people deal with eating disorders like bulimia.

Changing the way Pittsburgh's young people eat is high on her list of priorities, too. Bonci gets involved with various schools in her area and spends volunteer time with students promoting wellness and the prevention of diseases. Her association with the Steelers helps. Kids figure if the big guys listen to her, they might as well do the same.

Oceanographer

SKILL SET

✔ ADVENTURE

✔ MATH

✔ SCIENCE

GO visit marine life museums and aquariums.

READ about Jacques Cousteau's adventures.

TRY exploring sea life in your own bedroom—start an aquarium.

WHAT IS AN OCEANOGRAPHER?

Did you know . . .

- 💡 that the ocean covers more than 70 percent of the Earth's surface?
- 💡 that within the next 50 years, more than three-quarters of the U.S. population will live within 50 miles of the coastline?
- 💡 that the ocean and the seafloor provide important food, minerals, and energy resources for many parts of the world?
- 💡 that most international commerce is carried out by marine transport?
- 💡 that the ocean influences weather and is a part of the global climate system?

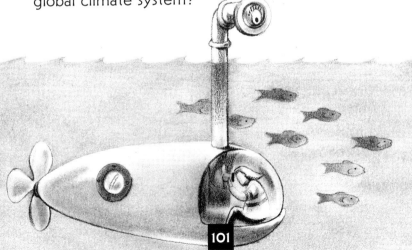

These are just a few of the issues that oceanographers work with every day. Oceanographers apply science and technology to the study of the ocean, its contents, and the surrounding environment through a combination of physics, chemistry, geology, biology, and engineering.

Unsolved questions awaiting the next generation of oceanographers include

- ☿ How can we continue to support growing populations near the oceans (with food, recreational resources, etc.) while protecting the coastal waters?
- ☿ What role does the ocean play in the development of major (and often devastating) storm systems?
- ☿ What kinds of structures can withstand severe storms?
- ☿ How can we best preserve and manage seabed resources such as cobalt, chromium, manganese, and platinum?
- ☿ In what way can the ocean help delay global warming?

There are various types of oceanographers, specializing in different academic disciplines:

Biological oceanographers study marine plants and animals.

Chemical oceanographers investigate the chemical composition of seawater and its interaction with the atmosphere and the seafloor. The study of trace chemicals helps explain how ocean currents move around the globe.

Geological oceanographers study the ocean floor and map submarine geologic structures to find out more about the history of the earth.

Physical oceanographers investigate the physical dimensions of the ocean such as temperature, density, wave motions, tides, and currents. They often focus on how the ocean interacts with the atmosphere to influence weather and climate.

Needless to say, many oceanographers work near large bodies of water—the Pacific Ocean, the Atlantic Ocean, the Gulf coast, and the Great Lakes. However, computers and other technology now make it possible to conduct research from laboratories in even the most remote, landlocked areas.

Employment opportunities range from oil and gas research to environmental protection. Other jobs are found in education and training, regulation enforcement, and advisory services.

Oceanography and other marine-related fields appeal to a wide variety of young people. They may seem glamorous and exciting, however, to get the full picture of these professions, you have to include the meticulous research and long stretches of data collection that are part of any valid scientific process. If the only impression you have of oceanography is what you've learned from television documentaries, you need to take a good look at this career before deciding if it's right for you.

 TRY IT OUT

ONE DROP AT A TIME

The following activity is adapted from an online experiment offered by Sea World/Busch Gardens. It's a great example of the meticulous research often conducted by oceanographers.

1. Use a stopwatch or clock with a second hand to time how long it takes you to take a shower or bath.
2. Use an empty gallon container to catch water from your bathtub. Time how long it takes to completely fill the container.
3. Divide the time it takes you to shower by the time it took the jug to fill to find out how much water you use for this daily task.
4. Repeat this process for each member of your family. Add all the numbers together to find out how much water your family uses every day to keep clean.
5. Work out a plan to reduce your family's water usage by 25 percent.
6. To get a more complete picture of how much water your family uses, find out how much is used for washing

clothes, washing dishes, and watering the lawn. Make a plan to conserve this precious resource.

STRAIGHT TO THE SOURCE

Where does the water in your house come from? Start at the tap and trace its path through pipes to the original water supply. You may need some help from your local city government or utilities company to find out all you need to know. Draw a map that illustrates the path you discover.

✔ CHECK IT OUT

🖱 ON THE WEB

DIVE INTO THE WEB

Get your feet wet learning about oceanography at these Web sites:

- ☿ Get entangled in Neptune's Web at https://pao. cnmoc.navy.mil/educate/neptune/STUDENT.htm.
- ☿ See if you can uncover the secrets of the sea at http://www.secretsatsea.org.
- ☿ Take a tour under the Pacific Ocean at http://seawifs. gsfc.nasa.gov/OCEAN_PLANET/HTML/oceanography_ flyby.html.
- ☿ Meet some women oceanographers at http://www. womenoceanographers.org.
- ☿ Find answers to all your water safety questions at http://www.boatsafe.com/kids.
- ☿ Link to fun and informative marine and oceanography sites at http://oceanlink.island.net and http://www .kidskonnect.com/Oceanography/Oceanography.html.

FORE OR AFT?

What do flags and knots have to do with oceanography? Both help keep people and property safe at sea. Since oceanographers spend a lot of time on water, knots and nautical flags are two things they need to know about.

Nautical flags are used on boats to communicate with other boats at sea. Learn about them at http://www.soundkeepers .com/kids/alphabet and http://www.marinewaypoints.com/learn/ flags/flags.shtml. Be sure to print out your name card using nautical flags at http://www.sailtrilogy.com/nameinflags.

Every sailor worth his or her salt knows how to tie a variety of knots. Following are Web sites you can visit to find step-by-step instructions. Grab a shoelace or some rope and get tied up in learning how at http://www.soundkeepers.com/kids/alphabet and http://www.cccoe.net/lifeatsea/student/knots.htm.

AT THE LIBRARY

SEAWORTHY BOOKS
Explore the ocean depths in books such as:

Dixon, Dougal, and Mike Benton. *Secrets of the Deep.* New York: DK Children, 2003.

Franks, Sharon Roth. *You Can Be a Woman Oceanographer.* Marina del Rey, Calif.: Cascade Pass, 2004.

Littlefield, Cindy A. *Awesome Ocean Science.* Charlotte, Vt.: Williamson Publishing Company, 2002.

Morrison, Marianne. *Mysteries of the Sea: How Divers Explore the Ocean Depths.* Washington, D.C.: National Geographic, 2006.

Nye, Bill. *Bill Nye the Science Guy's Big Blue Ocean.* New York: Hyperion, 2003.

Savage, Stevens, Ron Taylor, and Valerie Taylor. *Oceans.* New York: Kingfisher, 2006.

Vogel, Carole G. *Underwater Exploration.* Minneapolis, Minn.: Rebound by Sagebrush, 2003.

WITH THE EXPERTS
Cousteau Society
710 Settlers Landing Road
Hampton, VA 23669-4035
http://www.cousteau.org

Marine Technology Society
5565 Sterrett Place, Suite 108
Columbia, MD 21044-2665
http://www.mtsociety.org

National Association of Marine Labs
http://www.naml.org

Oceanography Society
PO Box 1931
Rockville, MD 20849-1931
http://www.tos.org

Scripps Institution of Oceanography
8602 LaJolla Shores Drive
La Jolla, CA 92037-1508
http://www.sio.ucsd.edu

Sea Education Association
PO Box 6
Woods Hole, MA 02543-0006
http://www.sea.edu

GET ACQUAINTED

Ben Halpern,
Oceanographer

CAREER PATH

CHILDHOOD ASPIRATION:
To be a mechanical engineer.

FIRST JOB: Working as a cashier
in a retail store.

CURRENT JOB: Project coordinator, ecosystem-based management of coastal marine systems.

Oh, the places you can go when you are an oceanographer trying to figure out how to keep the world's sea life healthy and protected. That's what marine ecologist Ben Halpern has discovered as he's traveled to places as far-flung as Indonesia, Australia, the Soloman Islands (way out in the Pacific Ocean near New Guinea), South Africa, and the Caribbean.

Of course, he doesn't hit the likely tourist spots when he travels. More of his sight-seeing is done underwater, scuba-diving or snorkeling his way through coral reefs to get acquainted with the local sea life. Halpern says that the travel is definitely one of the best parts of the job and has allowed him to see some of the most beautiful places on earth. He's quick to add that it has allowed him to see some of the world's ugliest spots too.

In the case of the Solomon Island, the underwater views went from best to worst within a couple miles. In one spot, he documented the ravages of an aggressive logging industry that for 20 to 30 years had stripped the area of trees and caused a sediment run-off into the area that all but destroyed the coral reef. The lagoon was smothered in one to two feet of gritty silt. There were very few fish, and it was a devastating sight.

Then just a couple miles away, Halpern found another coral reef that was just brimming with beauty—hundreds of coral species, huge schools of fish, even five or six species of sharks schooling around him. He says that the contrast between the two sites was extreme. It was like going from depressing to inspiring in a quick jaunt down the coast. Studying the two extremes helps him understand the effects of fishing, run-off, and other industry by-products so that scientists can better protect these invaluable natural resources.

SCREEN TIME V. SCUBA TIME

What most people don't understand, Halpern says, is that underwater exploration is just a small part of an oceanographer's work. He estimates that he spends just one to two months each year in water. The rest of his time is spent sitting in front of computers analyzing data, determining the impact

of certain factors on conservation, and figuring out what to do about it.

Luckily, both sides of the job are good fits for Halpern, who says that he spent his childhood in nature thanks to the enthusiasm of his mother (who was a high school biology teacher and natural historian). He admits that, as much as he loved science, he resisted majoring in it while in college. He planned to major in religion or psychology instead. But he soon discovered that biology came easily to him and that he found those classes the most fun.

Still, when he graduated from college with a degree in biology, he decided that he needed a break and spent three years as a computer network administrator. He wanted to make sure that biology was the right choice for him. Eventually, he discovered that he was spending so much time volunteering with the Nature Conservatory and the New England Aquarium that it was clear that biology and ecology was it for him.

ECOLOGICAL EDUCATION

Halpern says that if you want to be a scientist of any kind, you pretty much need to plan on getting at least a master's degree. If your experience is anything like his, you won't regret it. Halpern says he loved graduate school, even though it meant working on a huge research project that resulted in a 200-page thesis.

Halpern attended graduate school at the University of California in Santa Barbara, which he discovered to be a spectacular place to work and live. He's pleased that, now that he's earned his Ph.D. in marine ecology, he has managed to continue his work through the University's National Center for Ecological Analysis and Synthesis.

A WORD TO TOMORROW'S SCIENTISTS

So you want to be a scientist or oceanographer some day? Halpern says the best thing you can do now is to go out and explore. Find a beach, a forest, or a coastline and discover things that interest you. The most important thing is to find something you are excited about. He says that you can always find a way to make a job out of something you enjoy.

Pharmacist

SHORTCUTS

GO watch the classic holiday movie *It's a Wonderful Life*. Find out what could happen if a pharmacist made a mistake.

READ about Native American natural remedies and other homegrown cures.

TRY thumbing through a medical guide and pronouncing the names of some of the medicines (some of them are real tongue twisters!).

SKILL SET

✓ BUSINESS

✓ MATH

✓ SCIENCE

WHAT IS A PHARMACIST?

Pharmacist is a profession that makes frequent appearances in books about top careers for the future. With people living longer and an emphasis on keeping people healthy, opportunities for pharmacists continue to grow at a faster than average pace. Simply put, an increased demand for medicines results in an increased demand for pharmacists to supply them.

The origins of the word *pharmacy* can be traced back to the ancient Greek *pharmakon*, meaning a drug, poison, even spell or charm. However, the profession as we know it today made its debut in the United States in 1821 with the founding of the first American pharmacy college in Philadelphia.

With expertise in both the scientific and clinical use of medications, the pharmacist is an essential member of the health care team. To be successful, a pharmacist must blend a genuine interest in people and health with a commitment to provide professional, competent care. Computers make it easier for pharmacists to keep track of all the technical information required for the job. However, making that information meaningful and helpful to the many patients they see every day is a skill that must be learned. Educating patients is as much a part of the pharmacist's job as filling prescription orders is.

Typical aspects of a pharmacist's work include curing illnesses; eliminating or reducing symptoms; slowing a disease; preventing disease; diagnosing disease—with minimum risk and maximum comfort for the patient. The basic job description for a pharmacist might include duties such as dispensing prescribed medications, advising patients on their use and possible side effects, recommending over-the-counter drugs, and maintaining accurate records. Checking and double checking are a must when accuracy is often a life or death consideration.

Odds are that you've encountered a pharmacist in the last week or so. Statistics indicate that Americans make over 5 billion trips a year to the pharmacy and that it's not unusual for a pharmacist to see one member of every family in his or her community every week. Odds are even better that your encounter took place in a drug store or community pharmacy since that's where 6 out of 10 pharmacists work.

Other places where pharmacists work include

hospitals, where pharmacists work in the hospital pharmacy or practice in a specialized area such as nuclear pharmacy, drug and poison information, or intravenous therapy.

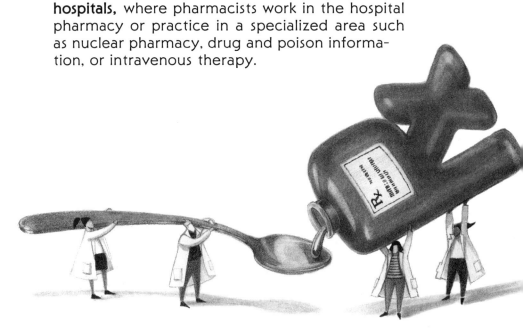

industry, where pharmacists work to develop new medications or manufacture health-related products.

government, where pharmacists work in a regulatory or public education capacity for federal agencies like the Food and Drug Administration or at the state level as pharmaceutical health inspectors or purchasers.

education, where pharmacists teach at the college level to help others prepare for a career in pharmacy.

A doctorate in pharmacy requires four years of professional study, following a minimum of two years of prepharmacy study after high school. It's rigorous but not quite as demanding as some other medical professions.

So, should you be a pharmacist? Here's how the experts at the American Association of Colleges of Pharmacy answer that question: "Yes. You should, if you seek a future in health services and patient care, a professional environment, and a rewarding career where you can use your talents and progress as rapidly as your ability merits."

☞ TRY IT OUT

WHAT'S IN YOUR MEDICINE CABINET?

With your parents' permission, go snooping in your family's medicine cabinet and make a list of all the medications you find there. On one side of your list, write the names of all the medicines that were prescribed to family members by a doctor. On the other, write the names of all the "over-the-counter" medications such as first aid ointment and pain relievers such as aspirin. Note the expiration date on each medication. Talk to a parent about discarding out-of-date and unnecessary medications. While you're at it, make sure that all medication is stored safely in a place where younger siblings or house guests cannot reach it.

RAINFOREST MEDICINE

Did you know that rainforests are full of medicines? It's true. Many of the plants found there have healing properties. Find out more about this medical magic at rainforest links found at http://www.rain-tree.com/schoolreports.htm.

To help organize your discoveries, draw a large tree or plant on a sheet of poster board and write the names of the plants and the ailments they are used to treat on different branches of your tree.

OH, MY ACHING HEAD!

Find the nonprescription medication aisle at the grocery store. First, look at all the aspirin-like medications. Note the different symptoms the medication is supposed to treat on the labels. See if you can determine the "magic ingredient" that makes each one work the way it does. Also, note the differences in dosage and prices. Make a chart to record your findings. If someone asked you for the most effective and least expensive remedy for a headache, what would you recommend?

✔ CHECK IT OUT

🖰 ON THE WEB

JUST SAY NO

The right drugs can help and the wrong drugs can hurt. Learn to tell the difference by learning all you can at these Web sites:

- ☼ Find out what you need to know about illegal drugs at http://kidshealth.org/kid/grow/drugs_alcohol/know_drugs.html.
- ☼ Chill out at the Cool Spot at http://www.thecoolspot.gov.
- ☼ Prove to the world that you're too smart to start at http://www.toosmarttostart.samhsa.gov/youth/youth.aspx.
- ☼ Dare to stay free of bad drugs at http://www.dare.com/kids/index_3.htm.
- ☼ Get the facts about illegal drug abuse at http://www.freevibe.com.

MEET THE PHARMACIST

The Web is a great source of information about what it's like to be a pharmacist, as you can discover for yourself at Web sites like:

- Kids Work! at http://www.knowitall.org/kidswork/hospital/realpeople/people/pharmacist.html
- A Day in the Life at http://www.princetonreview.com/cte/profiles/dayInLife.asp?careerID=111
- Career Voyages at http://www.careervoyages.gov/healthcare-main.cfm
- Dictionary of Occupational Titles at http://www.bls.gov/k12/science02.htm

AT THE LIBRARY

PRESCRIPTION FOR READING

Bone up on some background information about medicine and the medical profession with books such as:

Kidd, Jerry. *Potent Natural Medicines: Mother Nature's Pharmacy.* New York: Facts On File, 2005.

Powledge, Fred. *Pharmacy in the Forest: How Medicines are Found in the Natural World.* New York: Simon and Schuster, 1998.

Sohn, Emily. *Health and Medicine.* New York: Chelsea Clubhouse, 2006.

Rooney, Anne. *Medicine.* Chicago: Heinemann, 2005.

Silverstein, Alvin, and Virginia Silverstein. *Cuts, Scrapes, Scabs, and Scars.* Danbury, Conn.: Scholastic, 2006.

Townsend, John. *Medication: Pills, Powders, and Potions.* Chicago: Raintree, 2006.

WITH THE EXPERTS

American Association of Colleges of Pharmacy
1426 Prince Street
Alexandria, VA 22314-2815
http://www.aacp.org

American College of Apothecaries
Research & Education Resource Center
PO Box 341266
Memphis, TN 38184-1266
http://www.acainfo.org

American Pharmacists Association
1100 15th Street NW, Suite 400
Washington, DC 20005-1707
http://www.aphanet.org

American Society of Consultant Pharmacists
1321 Duke Street
Alexandria, VA 22314-3563
http://www.ascp.com

GET ACQUAINTED

Anthony Conte, Pharmacist

FIRST-GENERATION COLLEGE GRAD

Anthony Conte's father came to America as an infant with his brother and sister because their parents had died. Times were tough and they struggled to survive in their new country. Conte's father never had the opportunity to go to school, so he taught himself to read and write. He eventually owned his own business and made a nice living for his family. However, he learned to appreciate the value of an education and made certain that his only son, Anthony, made the most of his opportunities.

CAREER PATH

CHILDHOOD ASPIRATION: To become an engineer because he liked to draw mechanical illustrations of structures like bridges.

FIRST JOB: Started working in a pharmacy after school at the age of nine and stayed there until he graduated from high school.

CURRENT JOB: Mostly retired, occasional pharmaceutical consultant and painter of wildlife art.

It should come as no surprise that young Conte was first in his class in grammar school and high school. During his senior year, his father noticed a newspaper advertisement for a local university that said "become a professional pharmacist in four years." He decided that the program sounded like a good idea for his son, and fortunately Anthony agreed. Having spent several years working in a pharmacy—sweeping floors at first and gradually moving up to delivering prescriptions and helping customers—Conte liked the idea of becoming a pharmacist.

As it turns out, those early days in the pharmacy helped shape the pharmacist he would later become. One man in particular, Ray DiPiola, stands out as the ethical, generous person of principle that Conte worked to emulate in his own business dealings.

THOSE WERE THE DAYS

When Conte enrolled in classes at Long Island University's College of Pharmacy in 1948, tuition was just $422 per year. It cost him a nickel each way for transportation from his home to school and back.

Conte earned his bachelor's degree in pharmacy and went on to obtain a master's degree in pharmaceutical chemistry from Columbia University. He won an American Foundation Fellowship to pursue a doctorate at the University of Florida, but Uncle Sam preempted those plans with a military draft notice.

When Conte completed his military duty, he got married and opened a drug store in New York City in 1955. It just so happened that he shared a building with doctors that specialized in treating ear, nose, and throat problems. Located not far from Broadway, the doctors helped many famous stars keep their voices in shape for nightly performances. Conte eventually developed a special gargle that numbed the throat and reduced swelling in the membranes. It became a "voice-saver" for Broadway stars like Ethel Merman, Paul Newman, and Montgomery Clift.

NOW THAT'S SERVICE!

After being held up at gunpoint six times in seven months, Conte decided it was time to move out of the city. He found more than he had hoped for in Great Neck, New York. There he discovered a state-of-the art pharmacy that had been started by the Gilliar brothers in the 1920s. Offering home delivery by horse and carriage before there were roads in town, the brothers quickly made exceptional service the hallmark of their store.

The tradition of exceptional customer service continued under Conte's leadership, and the store was open every day of the year from 8:00 A.M. to 10:00 P.M. Conte made it a point to get to know his customers and to take the time to answer their questions about everything from health concerns to marital problems and financial decisions. His commitment to service even extended past working hours. It wasn't unusual to get a phone call at 1 A.M. or 2 A.M. from a frantic parent tending to a suddenly ill child. Conte never hesitated to open the store, fill the prescription, and deliver it even in the wee hours of the night.

Anthony Conte's "state-of-the-art" pharmacy

THE FAMILY THAT WORKS TOGETHER . . .

Conte often enlisted the help of his family in the store. His wife, Helen, also a pharmacist, worked behind the counter. His daughter, Lisa, became the resident cosmetologist, helping customers in the cosmetics department. His son, Charles, made deliveries.

This early introduction to the medical world paid off. Today, Charles is a surgeon, and Lisa is the chief executive officer of San Francisco–based Napo Pharmaceuticals, a company that develops, manufactures, and distributes life-improving drugs for a global market.

DON'T FORGET THE MATH

You can't do science without math, Conte advises. Skills like solving equations, making extractions, and drawing conclusions all come into play in the science of pharmacy. He also urges future pharmacists to do their homework by learning all you can about new medicines and treatments.

GET SOME RESPECT

During his many years in the business, Conte found pharmacy to be a well-respected and satisfying profession. He, like many other pharmacists, made a valuable contribution to his community and enjoyed helping the people in his neighborhood. A Gallup poll indicated that many Americans agree: For several years running, pharmacist has been named as one of the most respected professions in America.

Robotics Technician

WHAT IS A ROBOTICS TECHNICIAN?

Wouldn't it be great to have a robot that could clean your room, do you homework, and wash the dishes? So far, one with these skills hasn't been created, but you can be sure someone is working on it!

Robots are mechanical devices that perform tasks so that people don't have to; many *seem* to think like humans. Note that they only seem to think like humans. So far, people do the thinking for robots and must program their activity down to the most minute detail. Scientists and computer experts around the world are racing to be the first to develop a robot that can think on its own and make decisions. (Maybe you'll be the one to invent such a robot!)

Robotic technicians help engineers and other industrial scientists design, develop, produce, test, operate, and repair robots and robotic devices. In the field of robotics there are three specialties:

Artificial intelligence (AI) is the specialty in which scientists are attempting to find mechanical or electronic ways to mimic human intelligence capabilities. Scientists generally work in one of four general areas of research: pattern recognition, problem-solving, information representation, and natural language interpretation.

Technology is the specialty devoted to designing mechanical devices for maneuvering and manipulating. One of the goals of technology is to develop movement capabilities that function reliably and consistently without external control.

Computer programming is the specialty that involves teaching robots to communicate and follow commands. There's a smart computer programmer behind every smart computer and a smart computer behind every smart robot.

Many of the technological advances in this field have been in industries where robots are used to perform tasks once associated with assembly line labor, particularly in the automotive industry. Robots are often used to do work that would be dangerous, uncomfortable, incredibly boring, or even impossible for humans to do.

The best robotic technicians are scientifically minded and mechanically inclined. That's because the work can involve actually putting together very technical gizmos and keeping them running. Make sure to include some machine-shop skills and drafting with your math and science courses.

Whatever you do, make sure that any robots you work with adhere to Asimov's laws of robots. These three laws govern the ethics of robotic experts around the world.

☯ A robot may not injure a human being or through inaction allow a human being to come to harm, unless this would violate a higher order law.

- ❁ A robot must obey orders given it by human beings, except where such orders would conflict with a higher order law.
- ❁ A robot must protect its own existence, as long as such protection does not conflict with a higher order law.

 TRY IT OUT

CHORE BUDDY

You've been hired to help make every kid's dream come true by designing a robot that can help kids clean their rooms. Make a list of the tasks this robot must be able to perform. Then make a sketch of a robot with features that would allow it to do the job.

STRUT YOUR STUFF

Round up a few smart friends who like robots as much as you do, find a teacher to sponsor your team, and get ready to build a prize-winning robot to compete in contests such as:

- ❁ Botball at http://www.botball.org
- ❁ First Lego League at http://www.firstlegoleague.org
- ❁ First Robotics Competition at http://www.usfirst.org
- ❁ Robofest at http://robofest.net

 CHECK IT OUT

❁ ON THE WEB
MAKE IT HAPPEN

Behind every good robot is a manufacturing process that makes it work. Explore how manufacturing works at

- ❁ Manufacturing is Cool at http://www.manufacturingiscool .com
- ❁ Get Tech at http://www.gettech.com
- ❁ Dream It Do It at http://www.dreamit-doit.com

ROBOTS ONLINE

Go online to explore all kinds of robotic adventures:

- ☿ Introduce yourself to NASA's cool robot of the week at http://ranier.hq.nasa.gov/telerobotics_page/coolrobots.html.
- ☿ Find links to all kinds of online robots at http://ranier.hq.nasa.gov/telerobotics_page/realrobots.html.
- ☿ See how bomb squads use robots to diffuse bombs at http://www.pbs.org/wgbh/nova/robots.
- ☿ Get a grip on robotics at http://www.thetech.org/exhibits_events/online/robots/teaser.
- ☿ Learn how to build a robot using a Styrofoam meat tray at http://spaceplace.jpl.nasa.gov/en/kids/muses2.shtml.
- ☿ Still looking for information about robots? Find all kinds of interesting links at http://www.robotcafe.com and http://www.occdsb.on.ca/proj4632/kids.htm.

 AT THE LIBRARY

ROBOTIC READING

Read all about robots in books that include:

Brown, Jordan D. *Robo World: The Story of Robot Designer Cynthia Breazeal*. Washington, D.C.: Joseph Henry Press, 2006.
DK Publishing. *Robot*. New York: DK Children, 2004.
Gifford, Clive. *How to Build a Robot*. Danbury, Conn.: Franklin Watts, 2001.
Jefferis, David. *Artificial Intelligence: Robots and Machine Evolution*. New York: Crabtree Publishing Company, 1999.
Sobey, Edwin J.C. *How to Build Your Own Prize-Winning Robot*. Berkeley Heights, N.J.: Enslow Publishers, 2002.

WITH THE EXPERTS

Association for Unmanned Vehicle Systems
2700 South Quincy Street, Suite 400
Arlington, VA 22206-2242
http://www.auvsi.org

Robotics and Automation Society
Institute of Electrical and Electronic Engineers
Operations Center
445 Hoes Lane
Piscataway, NJ 08854-4141
http://www.ieee-ras.org

Robotics Industries Association
900 Victors Way, Suite 140
PO Box 3724
Ann Arbor, MI 48106-2735
http://www.roboticsonline.com

Society of Manufacturing Engineers
Education Department
One SME Drive
PO Box 930
Dearborn, MI 48121-0930
http://www.sme.org

GET ACQUAINTED

Richard Lefebvre, Robotics Engineer

CAREER PATH

CHILDHOOD ASPIRATION: He was intrigued by all things electrical and actually pursured a degree in electronics.

FIRST JOB: A stockboy in a hardware store during high school.

CURRENT JOB: Automation consultant and owner of R.L. Automation, LLC.

Richard Lefebvre got into robotics back in 1970—just when things started hopping. His work includes robotic advances in the areas of factory automation, systems integration, application engineering, and technical support. Since 1971, he has been directly involved in developing more than 600 welding and material handling robots. He named the first few, but after a while it was too hard to keep track of all of them.

HE'S GOOD AT WHAT HE DOES, REAL GOOD

In 1993, Lefebvre (out of every robotics engineer in the world) was named recipient of the Joseph F. Engelberger International Robotic Award for his impressive contributions to the advance of robotics in industry. The award is named after the father of robotics, the man credited with developing and patenting one of the first robots.

IT'S ALWAYS NEW

Lefebvre thrives on the challenge of his work. It is always changing, and he's learned to stay on top of new developments by reading journals, attending trade shows and conferences, and staying in touch with colleagues all over the world.

Lately, Lefebvre has focused on robotic laser cutting and has helped create a robot that can cut 150 features into an automotive frame as it moves through an assembly line. He says that the process they used to develop this technology is a lot like what happens if you take a magnifying glass outside, aim it toward the sun, and try to redirect the light to a piece of paper on the ground. If you get it just right, the light will burn a hole in the paper. That's essentially what the robot does using high-powered laser beams of light.

ADVICE TO THE NEXT GENERATION OF ROBOTICS PROS

Education, education, education. There's no way around it. The technology has become so sophisticated that a solid education is the cornerstone of success in this field. Learn how to learn and how to think things through; these skills can take you anywhere.

Lefebvre also encourages budding robotics engineers to channel their curiosity into science contests and robotics competitions. He says it's a great way to get comfortable with the technology and encourages robotic growth.

Science Educator

WHAT IS AN EDUCATOR?

That's a question you might be better qualified to answer than adults are. As a student, you are surrounded by educators every day. Classroom teachers, textbook writers, educational software designers, and more. If you stop and think about it you could probably write a job description defining the qualities of a really good teacher. You could probably write a pretty accurate description of a really bad teacher too—everyone seems to get their share of both.

As far as job opportunities go, education is a field in which things are expected to be booming as your generation enters the workforce. According to the U.S. Department of Education, overall school enrollment is projected to set new records every year until at least 2014. That means there will be plenty of opportunities in elementary and vocational schools, both public and private.

Colleges, vocational schools, and adult continuing education programs are other sources of teaching careers.

In addition, new technology such as educational software, the World Wide Web, and multimedia materials has created some interesting niches that provide educators with options in addition to actually teaching in a classroom.

Of course, there will always be a need for well-trained, highly motivated, committed teachers to work in classrooms

for all ages—preschool through advanced college degrees. The old saying that "if you can't do it, teach it" is completely out of sync with our modern world. The educational needs of modern society require instructors who are the cream of the crop in every way—as communicators, as subject experts, and as worthy role models.

This is how the American Federation of Teachers describes the job of teaching: "It's difficult, wonderful, exhausting, fun, stressful, enlightening—and rewarding beyond compare. Teaching requires enormous patience. Good teachers are fair to their students, they are interested in ideas, they believe that teaching and learning are important. They have a strong commitment to democracy and social progress. Good teachers want to make a difference."

Science teachers, in particular, tend to be a highly specialized group. The focus is generally on life sciences, chemistry, or physics. The older the audience, the more specialized the class content. For instance, in some high schools and in most colleges, instructors may teach courses in astronomy, genetics, or biochemistry. It is especially necessary that science teachers stay current in their fields by reading about new discoveries and theories in professional journals, participating in workshops and continuing education opportunities, and keeping up with technological advances.

So, what do you think? Are you ready to don a lab coat and introduce others to the mysteries of science?

☞ TRY IT OUT

PEER PRESSURE

Many schools offer peer counseling or tutoring programs that involve students in helping other students. Find out if your school or a nearby elementary school offers any programs like this and sign up for training.

Once you get a little older you may find that child care centers, recreation centers, and summer day-camp programs can be a great training ground for your teaching aspirations. Some public libraries also use young teens as assistants in programs that promote reading among children. Find out about volunteer opportunities or part-time jobs in programs that serve little people.

You'll learn more and enjoy the experience more if you link up with a good program. Ask your parents, a teacher, or a school counselor to help you check out the program's credentials and reputation before you commit yourself to spending time there.

Another option is to offer babysitting services to neighbors and relatives. Put together a bag of tricks to entertain the children, actually plan some interesting age-appropriate activities for your young charges, and watch your savings account grow with your earnings. (A hint from an experienced employer of babysitters: Clean up your messes and do the dishes; you'll get paid more and be asked back again!)

EXPERTS JOURNAL

Pick a topic that you'd like to know more about: clouds, ecosystems, something scientific. Find all the materials about this topic that you can (look in the children's section, young adult section, and general nonfiction section of the library; ask your teachers for suggestions; check out Internet resources). In short, become a miniexpert on your topic. Record your findings in a notebook.

Next, make a plan for how you could share this information in a way that would be meaningful and memorable to a younger audience. Make visuals, design experiments, and out-

line a verbal presentation. Put your lesson together in a way that you would prefer for your own school lessons—lively, fun, interesting. Get some neighborhood kids together or recruit your younger siblings and put your teaching skills to the test.

 CHECK IT OUT

ON THE WEB
SCIENTIFIC SURFING

Teach yourself some interesting stuff about science at these Web sites:

- ☼ Keep up with the latest science news at http://www.sciencenewsforkids.org.
- ☼ Turn on the light about the science of light at http://www.learner.org/teacherslab/science/light.
- ☼ Chill out at the cool science for curious kids Web site at http://www.hhmi.org/coolscience.
- ☼ Find science for kids at http://www.ars.usda.gov/is/kids.
- ☼ Get connected with science at http://www.ars.usda.gov/is/kids.
- ☼ Mix hot science with your cool ideas at http://pbskids.org/zoom/activities/sci.

AT THE LIBRARY

SCIENCE LAB IN A BOOK

Experiment with some scientific concepts with ideas you find in books such as:

Bardhan-Quallen, Sudipta. *Last Minute Science Fair Projects: When Your Bunsen's Not Burning But the Clock is Really Ticking.* New York: Sterling, 2006.

Hansen, Rosanna. *Discovery Channel Young Scientist Challenge: Taking Science to the Extreme.* New York: Jossey Bass, 2006.

Harris, Elizabeth Snoke. *Crime Scene Science Fair Projects.* Asheville, N.C.: Lark Books, 2006.

Mandell, Muriel. *No Sweat Science.* New York: Sterling, 2005.
Spangler, Steve. *Secret Science: 25 Science Experiments Your Teacher Doesn't Know About.* Sandy, Utah: Silverleaf Press, 2007.
VanCleave, Janice. *Great Science Project Ideas from Real Kids.* New York: Jossey Bass, 2006.

WITH THE EXPERTS

American Federation of Teachers
555 New Jersey Avenue NW
Washington, DC 20001-2029
http://www.aft.org

National Education Association
1201 16th Street NW
Washington, DC 20036-3290
http://www.nea.org

GET ACQUAINTED

Steve Spangler, Science Teacher/
Speaker/Inventor

CAREER PATH

CHILDHOOD ASPIRATION: A television game show host.

FIRST JOB: Disc jockey for wedding receptions and school dances.

CURRENT JOB: Nationally known science speaker, author, and lecturer.

If you ever get the chance to meet Steve Spangler, you'll never forget it. He's one of those guys who makes a lasting impression wherever he goes. He's funny. He's smart. He loves what he does. And it shows.

Spangler has two vocational passions, science and teaching, and he's found some exciting ways to combine the two into a truly unique career. Here's a list of some of the ways he does this:

- ☼ as host of the "Wonder Why?" science segment on *News for Kids*, a nationally syndicated children's television program
- ☼ as author of science activity books like *Taming the Tornado Tube: 50 Weird and Wacky Things You Can Do With A Tornado Tube!*, and *Down to a Science*
- ☼ as presenter of science assembly programs
- ☼ as creator of a popular line of science activities and science kits called Be Amazing! Toys
- ☼ as a trainer for teachers
- ☼ as leader of summer science camps
- ☼ Web site blogger at http://www.stevespanglerscience.com
- ☼ as director of the National Hands-on Science Institute in Denver

BLOOD AND GUTS

After his parents and teachers convinced him that there wasn't a big job market for game show hosts, Spangler started warming to the idea of becoming a doctor. He took all the right courses in high school and even landed a position as assistant to an ophthalmologist. He was on his way to hanging out a shingle that read *Steve Spangler, M.D.* The only problem—which he fortunately discovered sooner rather than later—was that he couldn't stand the sight of blood. This is a small but very significant detail for a doctor—time for plan B.

Spangler says that this experience taught him an important lesson that you need to know too: You never know if a career is right for you unless you try it! People learn best by doing!

THERE'S MORE THAN ONE WAY TO GET THERE!

Spangler graduated from college with a degree in chemistry. His plan was to start teaching at his old high school. Things were in upheaval at the school when he graduated, so his mentor advised him not to start teaching there. In fact, she advised him not to become a teacher at all but to consider becoming a chemist. Now what?

Spangler and his wife talked about the best next step. Spangler knew he didn't want to work as a chemist in a laboratory, so they looked at what he really enjoyed. Chemistry, teaching, magic, and interacting with people were high on the list. The next step was figuring out how he could make a living doing those things. The result was sending out brochures to schools offering to come in and "turn kids on to science."

Things took off from there—school presentations, the television show, the first books, the science camp programs—and Spangler had created his own custom-made career as a science "edutainer."

THE SQUIDY STORY

Spangler showed up on his first day of kindergarten with a science toy that he and his father had made for show-and-tell. It was something called a Cartesian diver—an eye dropper in a bottle of water that would float and sink simply by squeezing the bottle. Almost 25 years later, Spangler remembered his kindergarten experience and decided to use the floating and sinking eye dropper on his television program.

There was one unforeseen problem. The television camera had a hard time focusing on the eye-dropper—it was too hard to see in the bottle. After spending countless hours wandering around department stores and hobby shops, he stumbled across a device resembling a fishing lure that could be attached to the hard-to-see eye dropper. It made the eye-dropper look like a swimming squid. Spangler nicknamed it "Squidy" and took his idea back to his television producer.

Shortly after the segment aired on *News for Kids*, Spangler started receiving phone calls from viewers (mostly teachers) who were interested in purchasing "Squidy." Unfortunately, the rubber squidlike creatures that Spangler found in the fishing store were not quite big enough to fit over the eye dropper. So, he contacted a prominent fish lure manufacturer to see if they could make a special batch of rubber squid lures just for this experiment. After many confusing telephone conversations with the manufacturer (they couldn't understand anyone would want a fishing lure that wasn't intended to catch a fish!), they agreed on a price for the mold and the price of each rubber squid. The key, of course, was that Spangler had to purchase the little squids in quantity, as the manufacturer pointed out. How hard could it be to sell a few hundred Squidy Cartesian Diver toys?

Unfortunately, there was a communication breakdown on one tiny, little detail, and that was in the use of the term *quantity*. Steve assumed that quantity meant 500 or so. . . .

About three weeks after Steve placed the order, he found a surprise waiting for him on his driveway. It seems that a delivery truck dropped by earlier in the day and unloaded 80,000 rubber squids in boxes. Of course, with every delivery comes a bill—the bigger the delivery, the bigger the bill. Yikes!

It's one thing to come up with a clever idea for a science toy, but marketing and selling the toy proved to be the real challenge for Steve and his wife, Renee. After many months of hard work, a crash course in marketing and packaging, and frequent trips to trade shows around the country, Squidy had become one of the top selling science toys in the country.

Today, Squidy is available in over 1,000 stores and nearly 2,000 catalogs worldwide. It's a classic example of making lemonade out of the lemons life sometimes throws you!

THE SECRET OF SPANGLER'S SUCCESS

Spangler has been fortunate; throughout his life there have been special people who have helped guide him along the way. There was the ophthalmologist for whom he worked, his boss when he was a DJ, a very special teacher in high school, and wonderful parents who helped focus his energy. All these people took him under their wings, shared their experience, and taught him important lessons that helped prepare him for what he's doing now. Of course, the key to the success of these mentoring relationships was that he actually listened and used what he learned.

FAMOUS LAST WORDS

In his motivational presentations, Steve tells young people, "Don't tell me what you can do. Tell me what you love to do, and I'll tell you what you should do for the rest of your life. Take a risk and enjoy your success. Take a risk and fail miserably. Learn from every failure as you strive to reach your next goal. That's success!"

Veterinarian

WHAT IS A VETERINARIAN?

A veterinarian should have a love of animals, but it doesn't stop there. A veterinarian has to know as much about animals as a medical doctor knows about humans. In fact, the jobs are very similar. Animals get sick just like humans do. Animals get hurt in accidents just like humans do. Veterinarians are doctors who care for animals.

Most veterinarians care for companion animals, or pets, such as dogs, cats, and birds. Many run their own private clinics and carry the same responsibilities as other business owners and employers. In addition, a typical day at a clinic might involve immunizing a dozen dogs of various breeds, neutering or spaying a cat or two, performing emergency surgery on an animal that's been hit by a car, and setting some broken bones.

If the vet specializes in larger animals, his or her time might be spent at a farm, ranch, or zoo helping birth a new lamb, immunizing an entire herd of cattle, or giving nature a hand by artificially inseminating a horse. While most of their work is done during regular business hours, both types of vets must be ready to respond to middle-of-the-night emergencies.

Most of the routine tasks performed by a vet can be summed up in two categories: doing things to keep animals healthy—regular checkups, shots, and tests—and doing things to help sick animals get better—diagnosing diseases, prescribing medication, performing surgery, treating injuries.

While most veterinarians care for pets and farm animals in animal hospitals or clinics, other vets

- care for animals used in sporting events, such as horse races
- care for laboratory animals used in scientific studies
- care for zoo or aquarium animals
- specialize in areas like surgery, anesthesiology, microbiology, and pathology

Another option for veterinarians is public health work. These vets work for federal agencies like the Food and Drug Administration or the Centers for Disease Control, as well as state and local agencies. Some of the responsibilities of vets in public health might include

- protecting humans against diseases carried by animals
- inspecting livestock and foods
- conducting research and testing biological products such as vaccines
- evaluating new drugs to prevent or treat diseases in humans and animals

The major difference between private practice and public practice is the patient. In private practice the patients are individual animals or groups of animals with

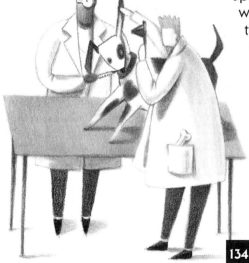

specific problems that the vet works to solve. In public practice, the patient is the entire community, and the vet's job is to safeguard overall health and well-being in simple and sometimes very complex ways.

For instance, one of the main tasks of the U.S. Department of Agriculture (USDA) is to protect people's food sources. This involves making sure that

food derived from animals is safe to eat and inspecting food processing plants. However, when an outbreak of some food-borne disease occurs (for example, an illness caused by E.coli), these veterinarians are among the detectives tracing tainted sources and remedying the problem.

Veterinarians must complete a rigorous college program to earn their doctorate degree in veterinary medicine. This training takes six to eight years to complete. Veterinary technician is another option that requires only a two-year associate's degree. Veterinary technicians assist vets in many ways including caring for hospitalized patients, conducting routine laboratory tests, taking X-rays, and assisting in surgical procedures.

Unlike the fictional Dr. Doolittle, most of the communicating that vets do is with people. They must be prepared to share the joy of a new litter of pups as well as the sorrow of euthanizing a dearly loved, hopelessly sick pet. It's important work. Just ask anyone who has ever loved a pet.

☞ TRY IT OUT

NOAH'S NOTEBOOK

Noah's flood lasted more than one night and so will this project. But, if you want to make animals the center of your career, you're going to have to start boning up on them. Get a three-ring notebook and some dividers. Stop and think before you do the next part.

How you organize will depend on how deeply you want to delve into the animal kingdom. You can divide the notebook according to categories of animals: companion animals (pets), large domesticated animals (farm and ranch animals), exotic animals (reptiles and birds), and zoo animals. Or you can get more specific with individual species: an entire section devoted to dogs, cats, horses, etc. You decide and get it organized.

Next, you'll want to find out all you can about these animals and write down the details. Find or draw a picture to include with each summary. Make sure to include information about feeding and breeding habits, life expectancy, and common personality traits.

The library, of course, can be a great source of information. Get online at the NetVet site and check out the Electronic Zoo for some fun information and photos (http://netvet. wustl.edu/e-zoo.htm).

Keep working on this project bit by bit until you've compiled as many animal facts as you can. Try not to get bogged down—after all it's just a notebook. Just think what it must have been like for Noah. You can bet that Noah sometimes wished all he had to take care of was a notebook!

ANIMAL KEEPER FOR HIRE

Get some firsthand experience caring for animals. You need to know how well you can handle the responsibility and how much you enjoy it. The experience will also help you when it comes time to apply to vet school; it is considered a plus. A few suggestions of where you could get some experience are

- ☿ at a pet store, vet's office, farm, ranch, horse stable, or zoo (be prepared for some of the dirty work—it comes with the territory) doing part-time work
- ☿ at an animal shelter on a volunteer basis or, if your parents agree, with an animal foster care program like MAXFund
- ☿ at a local 4-H group—most of these offer a variety of animal care programs

✔ CHECK IT OUT

🖱 ON THE WEB

SNIFF OUT INTERNET RESOURCES

You'll be hot on the trail of some fascinating information about veterinarians and animals at these Web sites:

- ☿ See what kinds of jobs veterinarians do at http://www.shrewsbury-ma.gov/schools/beal/curriculum/critterclinic/vetjobs.html.
- ☿ Find out what's behind animal behavior at http://www.pbs.org/wgbh/nova/vets.

☼ Visit the animal doctor online at http://www.vet.uga. edu/upp/animaldoc/index.php.

☼ Research some opportunities in animal research at http://www.kids4research.org/careers.html.

☼ Get some pet care tips at http://www.avma.org/ careforanimals/kidscorner.

☼ Find links to all kinds of Web sites about animals at http://www.kidsclick.org.

 AT THE LIBRARY

STRAIGHT FROM THE HORSE'S MOUTH

Find out more about what it's like to be a veterinarian in books such as:

Bowman-Kruhm, Mary. *A Day in the Life of a Veterinarian.* New York: Rosen, 2001.

Clemson, Wendy. *Using Math to be a Zoo Vet.* Milwaukee, Wisc.: Gareth Stevens, 2004.

Englart, Mindi Rose. *How Do I Become a Veterinarian?* Farmington Hills, Mich.: Thomson Gale, 2003.

Jackson, Donna, M. *ER Vets: Life in an Animal Emergency Room.* New York: Houghton Mifflin, 2005.

Marino, Betsy. *Emergency Vets.* New York: Dutton Juvenile, 2001.

Minden, Cecilia. *Veterinarians.* Chanhassen, Minn.: Child's World, 2006.

Parks, Peggy J. *Exploring Careers: Veterinarian.* Farmington Hills, Mich.: Kidhaven Press, 2004.

Patrick, Jean L.S. *Cows, Cats, and Kids: A Veterinarian's Family at Work.* Honesdale, Pa.: Boyds Mill Press, 2003.

Turner, Pamela S. *Gorilla Doctors: Saving Endangered Apes.* New York: Houghton Mifflin, 2005.

BOOKS FOR THE WILD AT HEART

Join five fictional characters who are volunteer workers at an imaginary veterinary clinic called *Wild at Heart* in some animal-loving adventures:

Anderson, Laurie Halse. *Fight for Life.* Milwaukee, Wisc.: Gareth Stevens, 2003.

——. *Homeless*. Milwaukee, Wisc.: Gareth Stevens, 2003.
——. *Manatee Blues*. Milwaukee, Wisc.: Gareth Stevens, 2003.
——. *Say Goodbye*. Milwaukee, Wisc.: Gareth Stevens, 2003.
——. *Storm Rescue*. Milwaukee, Wisc.: Gareth Stevens, 2003.
——. *Time to Fly*. Milwaukee, Wisc.: Gareth Stevens, 2003.

WITH THE EXPERTS

American Veterinary Medical Association
1931 North Meacham Road, Suite 100
Schaumburg, IL 60173-4360
http://www.avma.org

Association of American Veterinary Medical Colleges
1101 Vermont Avenue NW, Suite 301
Washington, DC 20005-3521
http://www.aavmc.org

North American Veterinary Technician Association
PO Box 224
Battle Ground, IN 47920-0224
http://www.navta.net

GET ACQUAINTED

Dr. Michael Blackwell,
Veterinarian

CAREER PATH

CHILDHOOD ASPIRATION: To be a vet.

FIRST JOB: Reopened his father's veterinary clinic in Oklahoma.

CURRENT JOB: Dean of the University of Tennessee College of Veterinary Medicine.

Wow! Dr. Michael Blackwell has enjoyed a distinguished career as a veterinarian. Not only has he owned and operated his own private practice, but he has also served as deputy director of the Center for Veterinary Medicine of the U.S. Food and Drug Administration (FDA), chief veterinarian of the U.S. Health Service, and Chief of State for the Office of the U.S. Surgeon General. He now serves as dean of one of the 28 veterinary colleges in the United States.

IN HIS FATHER'S FOOTSTEPS

Blackwell's father was a veterinarian, and Blackwell remembers following him around the clinic every chance he got from as early as he can remember. The only time he considered any profession other than veterinarian was in his senior year in high school when a career day recruiter enticed him with the notion of making big bucks with just a couple years of engineering training. It was tempting but not enough to lure him away from fulfilling his lifetime dream of becoming a vet. After graduating from college in Alabama, he returned to Oklahoma and doctored pets and farm animals in what had been his father's practice. Talk about tough shoes to fill!

NEVER SAY NEVER

After years of working directly with animals, Blackwell eventually reached the point in his career where he wanted to help people on a larger scale. Through an interesting series of events, he ended up pursuing a degree in public health, an aspect of the field he found so uninteresting while in vet school as to snooze through presentations about public practice opportunities.

As fate would have it, working for the FDA is where everything came together for him. He worked indirectly with animals, yet his work affected millions of people every day—even you. Now, as dean of a veterinary college, Blackwell is working to shape the future of veterinary education and the profession itself as it meets the needs of the public.

THE DAYS GET PRETTY LONG

Wearing as many hats as he does, Blackwell keeps on the run. Much of his day is spent solving problems. He serves on several national committees and in any given week can find himself at meetings in Washington, D.C.; Atlanta, Georgia; and Nashville, Tennessee.

He often represents the FDA at conferences with product manufacturers, veterinary associations, and animal breeders. It's important that he stays current in the field by reading journals and reports and by attending scientific meetings. He never seems to have enough time at his desk to do all the paperwork that continuously piles up.

LESSONS LEARNED

If Blackwell had a chance to do it all over again, there is just one thing he would change. He would have kept his options open as he went through vet school. Instead, he was so sure that he wanted to go into private practice that he didn't give serious thought to other opportunities. Especially in a field like medicine, where there are so many career tracks available, if you don't keep an open mind you might sleep through some great options.

AS EASY AS 1, 2, 3

Blackwell offers three tips for aspiring veterinarians.

1. Be realistic. If your idea of being a vet has only to do with cute, cuddly animals, forget it. Vets often deal with sick and injured animals. You have to be ready to deal with that reality.
2. Get experience working with animals. Find out if you like it and if you can stomach the tough stuff.
3. Work hard and get good grades. Even more important, make sure you really pick up the information you get in your classes (that's called learning). What you are learning now is a foundation for later in life. You'll need a strong foundation to make it through med school.

MAKE A SCIENTIFIC DETOUR!

Science is the foundation for many exciting career paths. This includes up-and-coming opportunities in environmental and technology fields as well as the tried-and-true fields of research, medicine, and the basic hard-core sciences.

It's pretty amazing to think about all the ways you could put your interest in science to work. The following lists include more than 100 scientific careers, and they barely scratch the surface of all the possibilities. These ideas are loosely grouped in categories to help you narrow down specific interest areas. Use them as a starting point to search out the best spot for your scientific interests and abilities.

To make the most of this phase of your exploration, draw up a list of the ideas that you'd like to learn more about. I'll bet there are at least three you've never heard of before. Look them up in a career encyclopedia and get acquainted with more possibilities for your future!

When you come across a particularly intriguing occupation, use the form on pages 160–161 to record your discoveries.

A WORLD OF SCIENCE CAREERS

HARD-CORE SCIENCE

This first category lists careers in some of the basic hard-core areas of science. You might be surprised to find introductory courses about these subjects on your list of course options at school. Connect what you are learning in school today with your future!

Also, you'll want to consider the full range of possibilities in each of these areas. Opportunities for technicians start with a strong high school science and math background and technical training and grow from there. In more sophisticated applications of science, advanced education is the key to increased responsibility, opportunity, and income. The following are careers in basic areas of hard-core science.

analytical chemist
biochemist
biologist
biotechnologist
cell biologist
geologist

geophysicist
microbiologist
mineralogist
molecular biologist
nuclear physicist
paleontologist

petrologist
physiologist
physicist
volcanologist

FRESH AIR, CLEAN WATER, AND OTHER BASIC ESSENTIALS

Growing concerns about issues such as pollution, global warming, wildlife preservation, and energy conservation make the environmental field ripe for scientists who want to make a difference. Many of these opportunities blend a knowledge of scientific principles with a sense of adventure and an interest in working outdoors.

Training requirements vary from job to job. This is an area where summer training programs abound. Get involved and explore all your options.

Here are some specific job titles to check out in detail.

air quality inspector
conservationist
ecologist
environmental
   scientist
fish and game
   warden
forester
forest ranger

hydrologist
inventor of uses
   for recycled
   materials
manufacturer of
   recycled products
park ranger
photovoltaic energy
   researcher

renewable energy
   and energy
   efficiency
   researcher
soil scientist
waste management
wildlife manager
wind energy systems
   engineer

CARING, CURING, AND CONQUERING DISEASE

According to a booklet published by the National Health Council, there are at least 300 ways to put your talent to work in the health field. The following lists some that are especially appropriate for the scientifically minded.

To obtain a copy of the booklet *300 Ways to Put Your Talent to Work in the Health Field* write the National Health Council at 1730 M Street NW, Suite 500, Washington, DC 20036-4505. This publication includes highlights of the health-related careers mentioned here as well as many, many more.

The following list of medical career ideas includes occupations requiring years of medical school and residency training as well as those requiring short-term or on-the-job training programs. As you consider these options, remember that any job can be the only stop on your career journey (you like it so much that you devote your entire life to it) or the first of many interesting stops. Start somewhere and go from there.

anesthesiologist
audiologist
bacteriologist
blood bank specialist
cardiologist
clinical chemist
clinical pathologist

cytogeneticist
cytotechnologist
dental assistant
dental technician
dentist
dermatologist
dietetic technician

EEG technician
endodontist
geneticist
gynecologist
histologic technician
licensed practical
   nurse (LPN)

nuclear medicine
technician
obstetrician
occupational
therapist
ophthalmologist

optometrist
pediatrician
periodontist
pharmacologist
physical therapist
physician assistant

podiatrist
radiologist
registered nurse (RN)
speech pathologist
surgeon

ON LAND, IN AIR, AT SEA

Oh, the places you can go with a scientific career! Don't overlook the option of working for Uncle Sam in one of the military branches (army, navy, air force, Marines, Coast Guard); there's great training and opportunity to be found on land, in the air, and at sea.

aeronautical
technologist
aquaculturist
aquatic chemist
astronaut
avian veterinarian
aviator
cartographist

fishery biologist
geological
oceanographer
hydrogeologist
hydrologist
ichthyologist
limnologist
marine biologist

marine geochemist
merchant marine
naval architect
navigator
oceanographic
technician
pilot
ship captain

BUGS, PLANTS, FOOD, AND FURRY THINGS

Work with life in all its forms is represented on this list. Some of these ideas require a full-fledged science education, others require a willingness to work hard and an openness to learn all that nature has to teach.

agricultural
climatologist
agronomist
beekeeper
biochemist
botanist
cattle rancher

dendrologist
dietitian
edaphologist
ethnobotanist
farmer
hydroponics
horticulturist

mammalogist
ornithologist
pedologist
silviculturist
viticulturist
zoologist

CRIME, GERMS, AND OTHER MESSY STUFF
You never know what you'll discover in some of these scientific endeavors.

coroner
criminalist
entomologist

epidemiologist
forensic scientist
immunologist

mortician
virologist

A WAY WITH WORDS
Keep your Skill Set in mind as you explore all your options.

health information specialist
health science librarian
science editor

science journalist
technical writer

A CREATIVE FLAIR
There are ways to combine a range of interests with science.

biophotographer
medical illustrator

science illustrator
underwater filmmaker

STILL SEARCHING FOR THE GREAT IDEA?
After all this, if you're still at that "I know I want to work in science, but I don't know how" stage, a great place to seek out general information is the American Association for the Advancement of Science. Its address is 1200 New York Avenue NW, Washington, DC 20005-3298. Make sure you also cruise by the association's Science Next Wave site on the Internet. The online address is http://www.aaas.org/careercenter/next_wave.

DON'T STOP NOW!

GO FOR IT!

It's been a fast-paced trip so far. Take a break, regroup, and look at all the progress you've made.

1st Stop: Discover
You discovered some personal interests and natural abilities that you can start building a career around.

2nd Stop: Explore
You've explored an exciting array of career opportunities in this field. You're now aware that your career can involve either a heavy-duty dose of science and all the educational requirements it may involve or a practical application of scientific methods with a minimum of training and experience.

At this point, you've found a couple careers that make you wonder "Is this a good option for me?" Now it's time to put it all together and make an informed, intelligent choice. It's time to get a sense of what it might be like to have a job like the one(s) you're considering. In other words, it's time to move on to step three and do a little experimenting with success.

3rd Stop: Experiment

By the time you finish this section, you'll have reached one of three points in the career planning process.

1. **Green light!** You found it. No need to look any further. This is the career for you. (This may happen to a lucky few. Don't worry if it hasn't happened yet for you. This whole process is about exploring options, experimenting with ideas, and, eventually, making the best choice for you.)

2. **Yellow light!** Close but not quite. You seem to be on the right path, but you haven't nailed things down for sure. (This is where many people your age end up, and it's a good place to be. You've learned what it takes to really check things out. Hang in there. Your time will come.)

3. **Red light!** Whoa! No doubt about it, this career just isn't for you. (Congratulations! Aren't you glad you found out now and not after you'd spent four years in college preparing for this career? Your next stop: Make a U-turn and start this process over with another career.)

Here's a sneak peek at what you'll be doing in the next section.

- First, you'll pick a favorite career idea (or two or three).
- Second, you'll link up with a whole world of great information about that career on the Internet (it's easier than you think).
- Third, you'll snoop around the library to find answers to the top 10 things you've just got to know about your future career.
- Fourth, you'll either write a letter or use the Internet to request information from a professional organization associated with this career.
- Fifth, you'll chat on the phone to conduct an interview.

After all that, you'll (finally!) be ready to put it all together in your very own Career Ideas for Kids career profile (see page 160).

Hang on to your hats and get ready to make tracks!

#1 NARROW DOWN YOUR CHOICES

You've been introduced to quite a few science-related career ideas. You may also have some ideas of your own to add. Which ones appeal to you the most?

Write your top three choices in the spaces below. (Sorry if this is starting to sound like a broken record, but if this book does not belong to you, write your responses on a separate sheet of paper.)

1. _____

2. _____

3. _____

#2 SURF THE NET

With the Internet, you have a world of information at your fingertips. The Internet has something for everyone, and it's getting easier to access all the time. An increasing number of libraries and schools are offering access to the Internet on their computers, or you may have a computer at home.

A typical career search will land everything from the latest news on developments in the field and course notes from universities to museum exhibits, interactive games, educational activities, and more. You just can't beat the timeliness or the variety of information available on the Web.

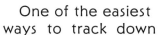

One of the easiest ways to track down this information is to use an Internet search engine, such as Yahoo! Simply type the topic you are looking for, and in a matter of seconds you'll have a list of options from around the world. For instance, if you are looking for information about companies that make candy, use the words *candy manufacturer* to start your search. It's fun to browse—you never know what you'll come up with.

Before you link up, keep in mind that many of these sites are geared toward professionals who are already working in a particular field. Some of the sites can get pretty technical. Just use the experience as a chance to nose around the field, hang out with the people who are tops in the field, and think about whether or not you'd like to be involved in a profession like that.

Specific sites to look for are the following:

Professional associations. Find out about what's happening in the field, conferences, journals, and other helpful tidbits.

Schools that specialize in this area. Many include research tools, introductory courses, and all kinds of interesting information.

Government agencies. Quite a few are going high-tech with lots of helpful resources.

Web sites hosted by experts in the field (this seems to be a popular hobby among many professionals). These Web sites are often as entertaining as they are informative.

If you're not sure where to go, just start clicking around. Sites often link to other sites. You may want to jot down notes about favorite sites. Sometimes you can even print information that isn't copyright protected; try the print option and see what happens.

Be prepared: Surfing the Internet can be an addicting habit! There is so much awesome information. It's a fun way to focus on your future.

Write the addresses of the three best Web sites that you find during your search in the space below (or on a separate sheet of paper if this book does not belong to you).

1. _____

2. _____

3. _____

#3 SNOOP AT THE LIBRARY

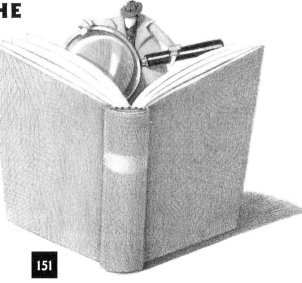

Take your list of favorite career ideas, a notebook, and a helpful adult with you to the library. When you get there, go to the reference section and ask the librarian to help you find books about careers. Most libraries will have at least one set

of career encyclopedias. Some of the larger libraries may also have career information on CD-ROM.

Gather all the information you can and use it to answer the following questions in your notebook about each of the careers on your list. Make sure to ask for help if you get stuck.

TOP 10 THINGS YOU NEED TO KNOW ABOUT YOUR CAREER

1. What is the purpose of this job?

   _____

2. What kind of place is this type of work usually done in? For example, would I work mostly in a busy office, outdoors, or in a laboratory?

   _____

3. What kind of time is required to do this job? For instance, is the job usually performed during regular daytime business hours or do people work various shifts around the clock?

   _____

4. What kinds of tools are used to do this job?

   _____

5. In what ways does this job involve working with other people?

   _____

6. What kind of preparation does a person need to qualify for this job?

   _____

7. What kinds of skills and abilities are needed to be successful in this type of work?

_____

8. What's a typical day on the job like?

_____

_____

9. How much money can I expect to earn as a beginner?

_____

10. What kind of classes do I need to take in high school to get ready for this type of work?

_____

#4 GET IN TOUCH WITH THE EXPERTS

One of the best places to find information about a particular career is a professional organization devoted especially to that career. After all, these organizations are full of the best and the brightest professionals working in that particular field. Who could possibly know more about how such work gets done? There are more than 450,000 organizations in the United States, so there is bound to be an association related to just about any career you can imagine.

There are several ways you can find these organizations:

1. Look at the "Check It Out—With the Experts" list following a career you found especially interesting in the Take A Trip! section of this book.

2. Go online and use your favorite search engine (such as http://www.google.com or http://yahoo.com) to find professional associations related to a career you are

interested in. You might use the name of the career, plus the words *professional association* to start your search. You're likely to find lots of useful information online, so keep looking until you hit pay dirt.

3. Go to the reference section of your public library and ask the librarian to help you find a specific type of association in a reference book called *Encyclopedia of Associations* (Farmington Hills, Mich.: Thomson Gale) Or, if your library has access to it, the librarian may suggest using an online database called *Associations Unlimited* (Farmington Hills, Mich.: Thomson Gale).

Once you've tracked down a likely source of information, there are two ways to get in touch with a professional organization.

1. Send an e-mail.

Most organizations include a "contact us" button on their Web sites. Sometimes this e-mail is directed to a webmaster or a customer service representative. An e-mail request might look something like this:

Subject: Request for Information
Date: 2/1/2008 3:18:41 PM Eastern Standard Time
From: janedoe@mycomputer.com
To: webmaster@candyloversassociation.org

I am a fifth-grade student, and I am interested in learning more about careers for candy lovers. Would you please send me any information you have about what people do in your industry?

Thank you very much.
Jane Doe

2. Write a letter requesting information.

Your letter should be either typed on a computer or written in your best handwriting. It should include the date, the complete address of the organization you are contacting, a salutation or greeting, a brief

description of your request, and a signature. Be sure to include an address where the organization can reach you with a reply. Something like the following letter would work just fine.

> Dear Sir or Madam:
>
> I am a fifth-grade student, and I would like to learn more about what it is like to work in the candy-lover profession. Would you please send me information about careers? My address is 456 Main Street, Anytown, USA 54321.
>
> Thank you very much.
>
> Sincerely,
> Jane Doe

Write the names and addresses of the professional organizations you discover on a separate sheet of paper.

#5 CHAT ON THE PHONE

Talking to a seasoned professional—someone who experiences the job day in and day out—can be a great way to get the inside story on what a career is all about. Fortunately for you, the experts in any career field can be as close as the nearest telephone.

Sure, it can be a bit scary calling up an adult whom you don't know. But two things are in your favor:

1. They can't see you. The worst thing they can do is hang up on you, so just relax and enjoy the conversation.

2. They'll probably be happy to talk to you about their job. In fact, most people will be flattered that you've called. If you happen to contact someone who seems reluctant to talk, thank them for their time and try someone else.

Here are a few pointers to help make your telephone interview a success:

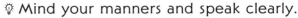

☼ Mind your manners and speak clearly.

☼ Be respectful of their time and position.

☼ Be prepared with good questions and take notes as you talk.

One more common sense reminder: be careful about giving out your address and DO NOT arrange to meet anyone you don't know without your parents' supervision.

TRACKING DOWN CAREER EXPERTS

You might be wondering by now how to find someone to interview. Have no fear! It's easy if you're persistent. All you have to do is ask. Ask the right people and you'll have a great lead in no time.

A few of the people to ask and sources to turn to are:

Your parents. They may know someone (or know someone who knows someone) who has just the kind of job you're looking for.

Your friends and neighbors. You might be surprised to find out how many interesting jobs these people have when you start asking them what they (or their parents) do for a living.

Librarians. Since you've already figured out what kinds of companies employ people in your field of interest, the next step is to ask for information about local employers. Although it's a bit cumbersome to use, a big volume called *Contacts Influential* can provide this kind of information.

Professional associations. Call, e-mail, or write to the professional associations you discovered using the activity on page 153 and ask for recommendations.

Chambers of commerce. The local chamber of commerce probably has a directory of employers, their specialties, and their phone numbers. Call the chamber, explain what you are looking for, and give them a chance to help their future workforce.

Newspaper and magazine articles. Find an article about the subject you are interested in. Chances are pretty good that it will mention the name of at least one expert in the field. The article probably won't include the person's phone number (that would be too easy), so you'll have to look for clues. Common clues include the name of the company that they work for, the town that they live in, and, if the person is an author, the name of their publisher. Make a few phone calls and track them down (if long distance calls are involved, make sure to get your parents' permission first).

INQUIRING KIDS WANT TO KNOW

Before you make the call, make a list of questions to ask. You'll cover more ground if you focus on using the five W's (and the H) that you've probably heard about in your creative writing classes: Who? What? Where? When? How? and Why? For example:

1. Whom do you work for?

   _____

2. What is a typical workday like for you?

   _____

3. Where can I get some on-the-job experience?

   _____

4. When did you become a _____?
   (profession)

5. How much can you earn in this profession? (But remember, it's not polite to ask someone how much *he* or *she* earns.)

   _____

6. Why did you choose this profession?

   _____

Use a grid like the one below to keep track of the questions you ask in the boxes labeled "Q" and the answers you receive in the boxes labeled "A."

Who?	What?	Where?	When?	How?	Why?
Q	Q	Q	Q	Q	Q
A	A	A	A	A	A
Q	Q	Q	Q	Q	Q
A	A	A	A	A	A

One last suggestion: Add a professional (and very classy) touch to the interview process by following up with a thank-you note to the person who took time out of a busy schedule to talk with you.

#6 INFORMATION IS POWER

As you may have noticed, a similar pattern of information was used for each of the careers profiled in this book. Each entry included:

- ☼ a general description of the career
- ☼ Try It Out activities to give readers a chance to find out what it's really like to do each job
- ☼ a list of Web sites, library resources, and professional organizations to check for more information
- ☼ a get-acquainted interview with a professional

You may have also noticed that all the information you just gathered would fit rather nicely in a Career Ideas for Kids career profile of your own. Just fill in the blanks on the following pages to get your thoughts together (or, if this book does not belong to you, use a separate sheet of paper).

And by the way, this formula is one that you can use throughout your life to help you make fully informed career choices.

CAREER TITLE _____

WHAT IS A_____ **?**
Use career encyclopedias and other resources to write a description of this
career.

_____

_____

_____

_____

SKILL SET

✔ _____

✔ _____

✔ _____

☞ TRY IT OUT

Write project ideas here. Ask your parents and your teacher
to come up with a plan.

_____

_____

_____

_____

_____

✔ CHECK IT OUT

ON THE WEB

List Internet addresses of interesting Web sites you find.

_____

_____

_____

_____

_____

📚 AT THE LIBRARY

List the titles and authors of books about this career.

_____

_____

_____

_____

🗣 WITH THE EXPERTS

List professional organizations where you can learn more about this profession.

_____

_____

_____

_____

GET ACQUAINTED

Interview a professional in the field and summarize your findings.

_____

_____

_____

_____

_____

_____

_____

_____

WHAT'S NEXT?

Whoa, everybody! At this point, you've put in some serious miles on your career exploration journey. Before you move on, let's put things in reverse for just a sec and take another look at some of the clues you uncovered about yourself when you completed the "Discover" activities in the Get in Gear chapter on pages 7 to 26.

The following activities will help lay the clues you learned about yourself alongside the clues you learned about a favorite career idea. The comparison will help you decide if that particular career idea is a good idea for you to pursue. It doesn't matter if a certain career sounds absolutely amazing. If it doesn't honor your skills, your interests, and your values, it's not going to work for you.

The first time you looked at these activities, they were numbered one through five as "Discover" activities. This time around they are numbered in the same order but labeled "Rediscover" activities. That's not done to confuse you (sure hope it doesn't!). Instead, it's done to drive home a very important point that this is an important process you'll want to revisit time and time again as you venture throughout your career—now and later.

First, pick the one career idea that you are most interested in at this point and write its name here (or if this book doesn't belong to you, blah, blah, blah—you know the drill by now):

_____

With that idea in mind, revisit your responses to the following Get in Gear activities and complete the following:

REDISCOVER #1:
WATCH FOR SIGNS ALONG THE WAY

Based on your responses to the statements on page 8, choose which of the following road signs best describes how you feel about your career idea:

- ♀ Green light—Go! Go! Go! This career idea is a perfect fit!
- ♀ Yellow light—Proceed with caution! This career idea is a good possibility, but you're not quite sure that it's the "one" just yet.
- ♀ Stop—Hit the brakes! There's no doubt about it—this career idea is definitely not for you!

REDISCOVER #2:
RULES OF THE ROAD

Take another look at the work-values chart you made on page 16. Now use the same symbols to create a work-values chart for the career idea you are considering. After you have all the symbols in place, compare the two charts and answer these questions:

- Does your career idea's **purpose** line up with yours? Would it allow you to work in the kinds of **place** you most want to work in?
- What about the **time** commitment—is it in sync with what you're hoping for?
- Does it let you work with the **tools** and the kind of **people** you most want to work with?
- And, last but not least, are you willing to do what it takes to **prepare** for a career like this?

PURPOSE	PLACE	TIME
TOOLS	**PEOPLE**	**PREPARATION**

REDISCOVER #3: DANGEROUS DETOURS

Go back to page 16 and double-check your list of 10 careers that you hope to avoid at any cost.

Is this career on that list? _____Yes _____ No
Should it be? _____Yes _____ No

REDISCOVER #4:
ULTIMATE CAREER DESTINATION

Pull out the ultimate career destination brochure you made (as described on page 17). Use a pencil to cross through every reference to "my ideal career" and replace it with the name of the career idea you are now considering.

Is the brochure still true? _____Yes _____ No

If not, what would you change on the brochure to make it true?

REDISCOVER #5:
GET SOME DIRECTION

Quick! Think fast! What is your personal Skill Set as discovered on page 26?

Write down your top three interest areas:

1. _____

2. _____

3. _____

What three interest areas are most closely associated with your career idea?

1. _____

2. _____

3. _____

Does this career's interest areas match any of yours?
_____Yes _____ No

Now the big question: Are you headed in the right direction?

If so, here are some suggestions to keep you moving ahead:

- ☼ Keep learning all you can about this career—read, surf the Web, talk to people, and so on. In other words, keep using some of the strategies you used in the Don't Stop Now chapter on pages 147 to 161 to do all you can to make a fully informed career decision.
- ☼ Work hard in school and get good grades. What you do now counts! Your performance, your behavior, your attitude—all conspire to either propel you forward or hold you back.
- ☼ Get involved in clubs and other after-school activities to further develop your interests and skills. Whether it's student government, 4-H, or sports, these kinds of activities give you a chance to try new things and gain confidence in your abilities.

If not, here are some suggestions to help you regroup:

- ☼ Read other books in the Career Ideas for Kids series to explore options associated with your other interest areas.
- ☼ Take a variety of classes in school and get involved in different kinds of after-school activities to get a better sense of what you like and what you do well.
- ☼ Talk to your school guidance counselor about taking a career assessment test to help fine-tune your focus.
- ☼ Most of all, remember that time is on your side. Use the next few years to discover more about yourself, explore your options, and experiment with what it takes to make you succeed. Keep at it and look forward to a fantastic future!

HOORAY! YOU DID IT!

This has been quite a trip. If someone tries to tell you that this process is easy, don't believe them. Figuring out what you want to do with the rest of your life is heavy stuff, and it should be. If you don't put some thought (and some sweat and hard work) into the process, you'll get stuck with whatever comes your way.

You may not have things planned to a T. Actually, it's probably better if you don't. You'll change some of your ideas as you grow and experience new things. And, you may find an interesting detour or two along the way. That's okay.

The most important thing about beginning this process now is that you've started to dream. You've discovered that you have some unique talents and abilities to share. You've become aware of some of the ways you can use them to make a living—and perhaps make a difference in the world.

Whatever you do, don't lose sight of the hopes and dreams you've discovered. You've got your entire future ahead of you. Use it wisely.

PASSPORT TO YOUR FUTURE

Getting where you want to go requires patience, focus, and lots of hard work. It also hinges on making good choices. Following is a list of some surefire ways to give yourself the best shot at a bright future. Are you up to the challenge? Can you do it? Do you dare?

Put your initials next to each item that you absolutely promise to do.

___ ☼ Do my best in every class at school
___ ☼ Take advantage of every opportunity to get a wide variety of experiences through participation in sports, after-school activities, my favorite place of worship, and my community
___ ☼ Ask my parents, teachers, or other trusted adults for help when I need it
___ ☼ Stay away from drugs, alcohol, and other bad scenes that can rob me of a future before I even get there
___ ☼ Graduate from high school

SOME FUTURE DESTINATIONS

Wow! Look how far you've come! By now you should be well-equipped to discover, explore, and experiment your way to an absolutely fantastic future. To keep you headed in the right direction, this section points you toward useful resources that provide more insight, information, and inspiration as you continue your quest to find the perfect career.

IT'S NOT JUST FOR NERDS

The school counselor's office is not just a place where teachers send troublemakers. One of its main purposes is to help students like you make the most of your educational opportunities. Most schools will have a number of useful resources, including career assessment tools (ask about the Self-Directed Search Career Explorer or the COPS Interest

Inventory—these are especially useful assessments for people your age). They may also have a stash of books, videos,
and other helpful materials.

Make sure no one's looking and sneak into your school
counseling office to get some expert advice!

AWESOME INTERNET
CAREER RESOURCES

Your parents will be green with envy when they see all the
career planning resources you have at your fingertips. Get ready
to hear them whine, "But they didn't have all this stuff when I
was a kid." Make the most of these cyberspace opportunities.

☼ Adventures in Education
http://adventuresineducation.org/middleschool
Here you'll find some useful tools to make the
most of your education—starting now. Make sure
to watch "The Great College Mystery," an online
animation featuring Dr. Ed.

☼ America's Career InfoNet
http://www.acinet.org
Career sites don't get any bigger than this one!
Compliments of the U.S. Department of Labor, and a
chunk of your parent's tax dollars, you'll find all kinds
of information about what people do, how much
money they make, and where they work. Although
it's mostly geared toward adults, you may want to
take a look at some of the videos (the site has links to
more than 450!) that show people at work.

☼ ASVAB Career Exploration Program
http://www.asvabprogram.com
This site may prove especially useful as you continue
to think through various options. It includes sections

for students to learn about themselves, to explore careers, and to plan for their futures.

☼ Career Voyages
http://www.careervoyages.gov
This site will be especially helpful to you as you get a little older. It offers four paths to get you started: "Where do I start?" "Which industries are growing?" "How do I qualify and get a job?" and "Does education pay? How do I pay?" However, it also includes a special section especially for elementary school students. Just click the button that says "Still in elementary school?" or go to http://www.careervoyages. gov/students-elementary.cfm.

☼ Job Profiles
http://jobprofiles.org
This site presents the personal side of work with profiles of people working in jobs associated with agriculture and nature, arts and sports, business and communications, construction and manufacturing, education and science, government, health and social services, retail and wholesale, and other industries.

☼ Major and Careers Central
http://www.collegeboard.com/csearch/majors_careers
This site is hosted by the College Board (the organization responsible for a very important test called the SAT, which you're likely to encounter if you plan to go to college). It includes helpful information about how different kinds of subjects you can study in college can prepare you for specific types of jobs.

☼ Mapping Your Future
http://mapping-your-future.org/MHSS

This site provides strategies and resources for students as they progress through middle school and high school.

☼ **My Cool Career**
http://www.mycoolcareer.com
This site is where you can take free online self-assessment quizzes, explore your dreams, and listen to people with interesting jobs talk about their work.

☼ **O*NET Online**
http://online.onetcenter.org
This U.S. Department of Labor site provides comprehensive information about hundreds of important occupations. Although you may need to ask a parent or teacher to help you figure out how to use the system, it can be a good source of digging for nitty-gritty details about a specific type of job. For instance, each profile includes a description of the skills, abilities, and special knowledge needed to perform each job.

☼ **Think College Early**
http://www.ed.gov/students/prep/college/
thinkcollege/early/edlite-tcehome.html
Even though you almost need a college degree just to type the Web address for this U.S. Department of Education site, it contains some really cool career information and helps you think about how college might fit into your future plans.

☼ **What Interests you?**
http://www.bls.gov/k12
This Bureau of Labor Statistics site is geared toward students. It lets you explore careers by interests such as reading, building and fixing things, managing money, helping people, and more.

JOIN THE CLUB

Once you've completed eighth grade, you are eligible to check out local opportunities to participate in Learning for Life's career education programs. Some communities offer Explorer posts that sponsor activities with students interested in industries that include the arts and humanities, aviation, business, communications, engineering, fire service, health, law enforcement, law and government, science, skilled trades, or social services. To find a local office, go to http://www.learning-for-life.org/exploring/main.html and type your zip code.

Until then, you can go online and play *Life Choices*, a really fun and challenging game where you get one of five virtual jobs at http://www.learning-for-life.org/games/LCSH/index.html.

MORE CAREER BOOKS ESPECIALLY FOR KIDS

It's especially important that people your age find out all they can about as many different careers as they can. Books like the ones listed below can introduce all kinds of interesting ideas that you might not encounter in your everyday life.

———————

Greenfeld, Barbara C., and Robert A. Weinstein. *The Kids' College Almanac: A First Look at College*. 3d ed. Indianapolis, Ind.: JIST Works, 2005.
Young Person's Occupational Outlook Handbook. 6th ed. Indianapolis, Ind.: JIST Works, 2006.

———————

Following are brief descriptions of several series of books geared especially toward kids like you. To find copies of these books, ask your school or public librarian to help you search the library computer system using the name of the series.

Career Connections (published by UXL)
This extensive series features information and illustrations about jobs for people interested in art and design, entrepreneurship, food, government and law, history, math and computers, and the performing arts as well as those who want to work with their hands or with living things.

Career Ideas for Kids (written by Diane Lindsey Reeves, published by Ferguson)
This series of interactive career exploration books features 10 different titles for kids who like adventure and travel, animals and nature, art, computers, math and money, music and dance, science, sports, talking, and writing.

Careers Without College (published by Peterson's)
These books offer a look at options available to those who prefer to find jobs that do not require a college degree and include titles focusing on cars, computers, fashion, fitness, health care, and music.

Cool Careers (published by Rosen Publishing)
Each title in this series focuses on a cutting-edge occupation such as computer animator, hardware engineer, multimedia and new media developer, video game designer, Web entrepreneur, and webmaster.

Discovering Careers for Your Future (published by Ferguson)
This series includes a wide range of titles that focus on adventure, art, construction, fashion, film, history, nature, publishing, and radio and television.

Risky Business (written by Keith Elliot Greenberg, published by Blackbirch Press)
These books feature stories about people with adventurous types of jobs and include titles about a bomb squad officer, disease detective, marine biologist, photojournalist, rodeo clown, smoke jumper, storm chaser, stunt woman, test pilot, and wildlife special agent.

HEAVY-DUTY RESOURCES

Career encyclopedias provide general information about a lot of professions and can be a great place to start a career search. Those listed here are easy to use and provide useful information about nearly a zillion different jobs. Look for them in the reference section of your local library.

Career Discovery Encyclopedia, 6th ed. New York: Ferguson, 2007.

Careers for the 21st Century. Farmington Hills, Mich.: Lucent Books, 2002.

Children's Dictionary of Occupations. Princeton, N.J.: Cambridge Educational, 2004.

Encyclopedia of Career and Vocational Guidance. New York: Ferguson, 2005.

Farr, Michael, and Laurence Shatkin. *Enhanced Occupational Outlook Handbook*. 6th ed. Indianapolis, Ind.: JIST Works, 2006.

Occupational Outlook Handbook. Washington, D.C.: U.S. Government Printing Office, 2006.

FINDING PLACES TO WORK

Even though you probably aren't quite yet in the market for a real job, you can learn a lot about the kinds of jobs you might find if you were looking by visiting some of the most popular job-hunting sites on the Internet. Two particularly good ones to investigate are America's Job Bank (http://www.ajb.org) and Monster (http://www.monster.com).

INDEX

Page numbers in **boldface** indicate main articles. Page numbers in *italics* indicate photographs.

A

activities, appealing   18–23
animal keeper 136
anthropology 30–31
Archaeological Institute of America 32
archaeologist **30–37**
artificial intelligence (AI) 118
associations, professional
    for archaeologists 35
    for astronomers   39, 42
    for chemists 49
    for engineers   56–57
    for food scientists 65
    for horticulturists   72–73
    for landscape architects 78
    for medical technologists 85
    for meteorologists   91–92
    for nutritionists   98–99
    for oceanographers 105–6
    for pharmacists   113–14
    for robotics technicians 121–22
    for science teachers 128
Associations Unlimited 154
astronomer **38–44**

B

Basri, Gibor 43–44
Blackwell, Michael   138–40
blood banks 81
Bonci, Leslie 99–100
books
    on archaeology 34
    on astronomy 41–42
    on all careers 151–52, 175–76
    on chemistry 45, 48